THE UNIVERSAL

SPELLING-BOOK;

OR,

A NEW AND EASY GUIDE

TO THE

ENGLISH LANGUAGE:

TO WHICH HAVE BEEN ADDED,

MURRAY'S ENGLISH GRAMMAR,

AND A COPIOUS

INTRODUCTION TO ARITHMETIC.

BY DANIEL FENNING.

DERBY:
THOMAS RICHARDSON AND SON;
SIMPKIN, MARSHALL, AND CO., LONDON.
1842.

1840

Roman Small Letters.

a b c d e f g h i j k l m n o p q r s t u v
w x y z.

Roman Capitals.

A B C D E F G H I J K L M N O P Q
R S T U V W X Y Z.

Italic Small Letters.

*a b c d e f g h i j k l m n o p q r s t u v
w x y z.*

Italic Capitals.

*A B C D E F G H I J K L M N O P Q
R S T U V W X Y Z.*

Old English Small Letters.

𝔞 𝔟 𝔠 𝔡 𝔢 𝔣 𝔤 𝔥 𝔦 𝔧 𝔨 𝔩 𝔪 𝔫 𝔬 𝔭 𝔮 𝔯 𝔰
𝔱 𝔲 𝔳 𝔴 𝔵 𝔶 𝔷.

Old English Capitals.

𝔄 𝔅 ℭ 𝔇 𝔈 𝔉 𝔊 ℌ ℑ 𝔍 𝔎 𝔏 𝔐 𝔑 𝔒
𝔓 𝔔 ℜ 𝔖 𝔗 𝔘 𝔙 𝔚 𝔛 𝔜 ℨ

Vowels.

a e i o u, and w y for u i.

Consonants.

b c d f g h j k l m n p q r s t v w x y z

Letters joined together.

fi, ff, fl, ffi, ffl, &, æ, œ.

N. B. I humbly desire all masters and mistresses never to let a child know there are two *i*'s or two *u*'s; but let them teach the child to call the long *j* [ja] and the sharp *v* [vee], for it is much better in every respect.

PART I.

TABLE I.

ba	be	bi	bo	bu	ab	eb	ib	ob	ub
ca	ce*	ci*	co	cu	ac	ec	ic	oc	uc
da	de	di	do	du	ad	ed	id	od	ud
fa	fe	fi	fo	fu	af	ef	if	of	uf
ka	ke	ki	ko	ku	am	em	im	om	um
la	le	li	lo	lu	al	el	il	ol	ul
ma	me	mi	mo	mu	an	en	in	on	un
na	ne	ni	no	nu	ar	er	ir	or	ur
ra	re	ri	ro	ru	as	es	is	os	us
sa	se	si	so	su	ax	ex	ix	ox	ux

bla	ble	bli	blo	blu	bra	bre	bri	bro	bru
cla	cle	cli	clo	clu	cra	cre	cri	cro	cru
pla	ple	pli	plo	plu	pra	pre	pri	pro	pru
sla	sle	sli	slo	slu	tra	tre	tri	tro	tru

fra	fre	fri	fro	fru	fry
phra	phre	phri	phro	phru	phry

PROPER WORDS OF ONE SYLLABLE, BOTH NATURAL AND EASY TO SPELL AND READ.

all	be	the	my	no	of	or	two
am	he	thee	thy	nor	off	so	up
and	me	ye	do	not	from	to	us
are	we	by	go	lot	on	too	you

* Let the child be taught to pronounce *ce* the same as *se*, and *ci* the same as *si*.

TABLE II.

MORE EASY LESSONS IN WORDS OF ONE SYLLABLE, ALIKE IN SOUND, NATURAL TO THE EAR, AND EASY TO SPELL AND PRONOUNCE.

1				3			
All	call	fall	tall	Bat	cat	hat	rat
ake	cake	make	wake	ben	den	hen	men
art	cart	dart	smart	car	bar	far	tar
are	care	hare	mare	cock	dock	lock	mock
ark	bark	dark	mark	clock	block	flock	shock
2				4			
Cap	gap	map	tap	Band	hand	land	sand
dip	hip	nip	pip	bail	hail	pail	nail
fan	man	nan	pan	book	cook	hook	look
got	hot	pot	sot	hope	mope	pope	rope
din	fin	sin	tin	lace	mace	pace	race
ink	link	pink	wink	make	rake	sake	wake

TABLE III.

EASY LESSONS OF ONE SYLLABLE, OF THINGS MOST NATURAL AND COMMON TO CHILDREN.

1. BIRDS, BEASTS, AND INSECTS.

Cat*	hog	bat	cock	lark	ant
dog	horse	crane	hen	owl	bug
cow	mare	crow	hawk	rook	flea
calf	colt	dove	kite	snipe	frog

2. OF PLAY, AND TERMS USED AT PLAY.

Ball	cards	gigs	play	tops	whip
bat	dice	leap	kite	trap	lose
cat	chuck	jump	spin	taw	win

* I have not regarded the order of the Alphabet in this Table, but have put such things first as are easy, natural, and most connected together; and they are to be taught downwards, not across, viz. cat dog, cow, &c.

3. EATABLES, ETC.

Ale	bread	buns	beef	fish	milk
beer	cheese	cakes	lamb	flesh	cream
rum	crumb	pies	pork	beans	curds
wine	crust	tarts	veal	peas	whey

4. APPAREL.

Cap	coat	fan	hoop	shoes	sloth
hat	cloak	gloves	knot	clogs	stuff
slip	frock	lace	scarf	shirt	plush
frill	gown	muff	stays	shift	silk

5. THINGS BELONGING TO A HOUSE.

Cup	clock	bench	broom	pap	brick
dish	door	box	brush	pot	lime
knife	bar	chest	chair	bed	stone
fork	bolt	trunk	stool	couch	tiles
spoon	latch	grate	shelf	quilt	slate
plate	lock	jack	glass	rug	thatch
mug	key	spit	stairs	sheet	roof

6. PARTS OF THE BODY.

Head	scull	cheeks	back	toes	heart
hair	brain	throat	bones	nails	lungs
face	lips	arms	ribs	shins	vein
eyes	tongue	hand	knees	thumb	blood
nose	teeth	breast	legs	fist	nerves
mouth	chin	ears	feet	wrist	joints

7. THE WORLD.

Sun	east	cape	clay	brook	frost
moon	west	rock	dirt	pool	snow
stars	north	land	bank	pond	mist
air	south	hill	sand	rain	dew
wind	earth	isle	chalk	hail	ice

8. TREES, PLANTS, FRUIT, &c.

Ash	fir	broom	hops	oats	pears
bay	lime	hemp	reeds	rye	plums
beech	oak	flax	rose	wheat	grapes
birch	pine	fern	rue	crabs	leaf
box	vine	grass	sage	figs	roots
elm	yew	herbs	shrub	nuts	trees

9. NUMBER, WEIGHT, &c.

One	five	nine	grain	inch	drop
two	six	ten	ounce	foot	dram
three	sev'n*	once	pound	yard	pint
four	eight	twice	score	ell	quart

10. TITLES AND NAMES.

King	duke	peer	wife	aunt	Mark
queen	earl	knight	child	niece	Luke
prince	lord	page	son	bride	John

* Rather than break the Order of Number, I have (for the Child's sake) taken the liberty to spell the word "seven" in one Syllable.

TABLE IV.

EASY LESSONS IN WORDS* OF ONE SYLLABLE, BY WHICH A CHILD WILL SOONER KNOW BOTH THE SOUND AND USE OF e FINAL. TO BE READ, al, ale,—ar, are, &c.

Al	ale	bil	bile	cor	core	dot	dote
ar	are	bit	bite	dal	dale	fam	fame
at	ate	can	cane	dam	dame	fan	fane
bab	babe	cam	came	dan	dane	far	fare
bal	bale	car	care	dar	dare	fat	fate
ban	bane	cap	cape	dat	date	fil	file
bar	bare	col	cole	din	dine	fin	fine
bas	base	con	cone	dol	dole	fir	fire
bid	bide	cop	cope	dom	dome	for	fore

* I here use the term *word*, not in its strict and confined sense, as signifying something that has a meaning, but in its more general and enlarged sense, as implying any thing that has an articulate sound.

gal	gale	mir	mire	por	pore	tam	tame
gam	game	mod	mode	rat	rate	tap	tape
gap	gape	mol	mole	rid	ride	tar	tare
gat	gate	mop	mope	rip	ripe	tid	tide
gaz	gaze	mor	more	rit	rite	til	tile
gor	gore	mut	mute	rob	robe	tim	time
hal	hale	nam	name	rod	rode	tin	tine
har	hare	nap	nape	rop	rope	ton	tone
hat	hate	nil	nile	rot	rote	top	tope
her	here	nod	node	rud	rude	tub	tube
hid	hide	nor	nore	rul	rule	tun	tune
hop	hope	not	note	sal	sale	us	use
kin	kine	od	ode	sam	same	val	vale
kit	kite	or	ore	sid	side	van	vane
lad	lade	pan	pane	sin	sine	vil	vile
mad	made	par	pare	sir	sire	vin	vine
man	mane	pat	pate	sit	site	vot	vote
mar	mare	pil	pile	sol	sole	wad	wade
mat	mate	pin	pine	sur	sure	war	ware
mil	mile	pol	pole	tal	tale	win	wine

TABLE V.

LESSONS IN WORDS OF ONE SYLLABLE, VERY EASY TO SPELL AND READ, AND BY WHICH A CHILD MAY BEGIN TO KNOW HIS DUTY TO GOD AND MAN.

*** If any of the following lessons be too long, they are so ordered that the child may spell and read only a part of them, according to his capacity, or the direction of his master.

LESSON I.

Be a good child.
Love and fear God.
Mind your book.
Love your school.

Strive to learn.
Tell no tales.
Call no ill names.
Pay to God his due.

LESSON II.

Do as you are bid
Do not lie nor swear.
Do not cheat nor steal.
Do all that is just.
Play not with bad boys.
Serve God, and trust in him.
Pray God to bless you.

LESSON III.

My good child, walk not in thine own way, but in the ways of the Lord.

Spend your time well, and God will bless you; he will love you, and do you good.

LESSON IV.

Go not far from me, O Lord; but be with me, and help me, O my God.

I will not play with them that do ill; for if I do, the Lord will not love me.

LESSON V.

I will love thee, O Lord; for thou hast made me, and art kind to me in all things.

Day by day will I praise thee; I will not play with them that take thy name in vain.

Keep me, O Lord, from such as love not thy law, and walk not in thy ways.

LESSON VI.

The eye of the Lord is on them that fear him, and that put their trust in him.

He will bless them that fear him; he will love them, and do them good.

As for such as love not the way of the Lord, he will hide his face from them, and will not save them, but they shall go down to the pit.

OF THE CREATION.

By the word of the Lord were all things made. God made the world; he made both man and beast. He made the fowls of the air, and the fish of the sea.

He made the Sun to rule the Day, and the Moon and Stars to rule the Night. How great are thy works, O Lord!

DUTY TO GOD.

Thou shalt love the Lord thy God with all thy heart, with all thy soul, with all thy mind, and with all thy strength.

A good child will love God: he will put his whole trust in him: he will call on him, he will love his name and his word; and he will serve him and fear him all the days of his life.

OF GOD.

The fool says in his heart, There is no God: but a wise and good man knows that there is a God, and that the Lord he is God.

God is our Lord, he is King of kings, and Lord of lords. Who is like the Lord our God? There is none like the Lord our God.

OF GOD'S ATTRIBUTES.

The Lord God will be our Judge. God is a true, wise, and just God; he plants, he builds, and he lifts up: for the word of the Lord is true, and it shall come to pass.

All things change; but God says, I change not, I am the same God, I have no end. There is but one true God. The Lord our God is one Lord: the Lord of hosts is his name.

OF CHRIST OUR REDEEMER.

Christ is God as well as man. The Word was with God, and the word was God. Christ is the way, the truth, and the life: and none can come to God but by Christ; for he took upon him the form of man.

Christ was made man to save us from the wrath to come. He was made poor for our sakes. He is the Prince of the kings of the earth: and he shall judge the quick and the dead at last: the Lord of Hosts is his name.

OF THE CHILD'S DUTY TO HIMSELF AND OTHERS.

A good child will not lie, swear, nor steal, nor will he take God's name in vain. He will be good at home, and will be careful to read his book; and when he gets up, he will wash his face and hands clean, comb out his hair, and make haste to school, and will not play by the way as bad boys do.

When a good boy is at school he will mind his book, and try to learn to spell and read well, and not play in school-time; and when he goes to, or comes from school, he will pull off his hat, or bow to all he meets; and when he goes to church, he will sit, kneel, or stand still; and when he comes home, he will read God's word, or some good book, that God may bless him.

As for that boy that minds not his church, his school, nor his book, but plays with such boys as tell tales, tell lies, swear, steal, and take God's name in vain, he will come to some ill end, if he be not well whipt at school, and at home, day and night, till he leaves off such things.

A TRIAL OF CAPITALS.

HE THAT LOVES GOD, HIS SCHOOL, AND HIS BOOK, WILL NO DOUBT DO WELL AT LAST: BUT HE THAT HATES HIS SCHOOL AND HIS BOOK, WILL LIVE AND DIE A SLAVE, A FOOL, AND A DUNCE.

TABLE VI.

WORDS OF TWO SYLLABLES, ACCENTED ON THE FIRST SYLLABLE.

Ab-bot	cham-ber	doc-trine	fol-ly
ab-bey	chan-nel	drum-mer	fop-pish
ac-tor	chap-man	drunk-ard	for-est
ad-vent	ohap-ter	dung-hill	for-ty
af-ter	chat-ter	du-ty	found-ling
al-um	chest-nut	dy-er	fret-ful
am-ber	child-ish	El-bow	fro-ward
an-gel	chil-dren	em-bers	fro-zen
ar-bour	cler-gy	em-blem	fru-gal
art-ful	cof-fin	en-ter	fu-el
art-less	col-lect	e-vil	fun-nel
Back-ward	com-fort	Fac-tor	fur-long
ba-ker	com-ment	fag-ot	Gal-lon
bal-lad	com-merce	fan-cy	gal-lop
bank-er	com-mon	fan-tom	game-ster
bant-ling	con-cord	farm-er	gam-mon
bar-ber	con-quer	fa-tal	gan-der
bar-rel	con-quest	fat-ling	gar-den
bash-ful	con-sul	fe-male	gar-land
bet-ter	con-trite	fen-der	gar-ment
bit-ter	cor-ner	fen-nel	gar-ret
blun-der	cost-ly	fe-ver	gar-ter
bor-der	craf-ty	fid-dler	gen-try
bri-er	cra-zy	fil-let	gi-ant
brim-stone	cru-el	fi-nal	gib-bet
bro-ken	cum-ber	fi-ring	gip-sy
bus-kin	cut ler	flan-nel	glim-mer
but-ter	Dar-ling	flat-ter	glit-ter
Cab-bage	di-al	floun-der	glo-ry
ca-per	di-et	flu-ent	glut-ton
car-rot	din-ner	fod-der	god-ly
car-ter	doc-tor	fog-gy	gold-finch

gos-pel
grate-ful
gras-sy
grace-ful
gra-vy
grit-ty
gru-el
gul-let
gun-ner
gun-shot
gut-ter
Ham-let
ham-mer
hand-ful
han-dy
hang-er
hang-ings
hap-py
hard-ship
har-dy
har-lot
har-per
harts-horn
har-vest
ha-sty
hatch-et
help-ful
her-mit
hin-der
hin-drance
ho-ly
home-ly
hope-ful
hor-net
hor-rid

horse-man
host-ler
hun-dred
hunt-er
hurt-ful
hus-band
I-cy
i-dol
in-fant
in-sect
in-side
in-stance
in-step
in-ward
i-vy
Jest-er
joc-key
jol-ly
judge-ment
ju-ry
Ken-nel
ker-nel
kin-dred
king-dom
kins-man
kitch-en
Lad-der
la-dy
land-lord
land-mark
land-scape
lap-pet
lap-wing
la-zy
le-gal

let-ter
like-ly
lim-ber
lin-net
li-on
lit-ter
lof-ty
lord-ly
lord-ship
luc-ky
lug-gage
Ma-ker
mam-mon
man-ful
man-ly
man-na
man-ner
ma-ny
mar-gin
mar-ket
ma-tron
max-im
med-ley
mem-ber
mer-cy
mer-ry
mil-ler
mit-tens
mo-dish
mo-ment
morn-ing
mor-tal
mot-to
mud-dy
mur-der

mur-mur
mut-ter
Nap-kin
nim-ble
nine-ty
num-ber
nut-meg
Of-fer
of-fice
on-set
or-der
or-gan
Pa-gan
pam-per
pan-nel
pan-try
pa-per
pa-pist
par-don
pa-rents
par-lour
par-rot
part-ner
par-ty
pat-tern
pave-ment
pen-cil
pen-ny
pep-per
per-fect
per-son
pic-ture
pil-grim
pil-lar
pi-lot

pi-per	ru-ral	shil-ling	spite-ful
pip-kin	Sa-cred	short-ly	splen-did
po-et	sad-dler	shut-ter	splen-dour
pos-set	safe-ly	sig-nal	splin-ter
pot-ter	safe-ty	si-lence	spun-gy
pre-cept	sal-ad	si-lent	stag-ger
pru-dent	sal-ver	sil-ly	stam-mer
pup-py	san-dy	sil-ver	stand-ish
pur-blind	sam-pler	sim-per	stin-gy
pur-chase	satch-el	sin-ful	stop-page
pur-pose	sat-in	sin-ner	stop-per
Quar-rel	scab-bard	six-fold	sto-ry
quar-ter	scaf-fold	six-ty	stran-ger
qui-et	scam-per	skil-ful	strong-ly
Rab-bit	scan-dal	skin-ny	stu-dent
rag-ged	scan-ty	skip-per	stu-pid
ra-ker	scar-let	slan-der	sud-den
ram-mer	scat-ter	slat-tern	suf-fer
ran-dom	scol-lop	slen-der	sul-ky
ran-som	scorn-ful	sli-my	sul-len
ran-ger	scra-per	slip-per	sul-ly
rant-er	scul-ler	sloth-ful	sul-try
rec-tor	se-cret	slug-gard	sum-mer
rem-nant	sel-dom	slug-gish	sum-mon
ren-der	self-ish	slum-ber	sup-per
ri-der	sen-tence	slut-tish	sur-face
ri-ot	ser-mon	smo-ky	sur-ly
rob-ber	ser-vant	smug-gler	Tab-by
rub-bish	sex-ton	snap-pish	tal-ly
ru-by	sha-dy	so-ber	tame-ly
rug-ged	shame-ful	sor-rel	tan-ner
ru-in	sharp-en	sot-tish	ta-per
ru-ler	sharp-er	spi-der	tap-ster
rum-mage	shat-ter	spin-ner	tar-dy
run-ner	shep-herd	spin-ster	tar-nish

tat-ler	trum-pet	ves-sel	ward-robe
tat-ter	trus-ty	vic-tim	war-like
tem-per	tu-lip	vin-tage	war-rant
tem-pest	tum-bler	vir-gin	wasp-ish
ten-der	tu-mult	vi-tal	waste-ful
ten-ter	tur-key	vo-cal	wed-ding
thank-ful	tur-nip	vul-gar	wel-fare
thread-bare	turn-er	Ud-der	wet-shod
thun-der	turn-pike	ug-ly	whim-sey
time-ly	turn-stile	up-per	whis-per
ti-dings	tu-tor	ut-most	wis-dom
tim-ber	va-cant	ut-ter	wil-ful
tin-der	va-grant	use-ful	win-ter
tin-sel	var-nish	Wa-fer	wo-ful
ton-nage	va-ry	wa-ger	wood-land
to-tal	vel-lum	wa-ges	wor-ship
tra-der	vel-vet	wake-ful	worth-less
trench-er	ven-ture	wan-der	wor-thy
tri-al	ver-min	wan-ton	won-der

TABLE VII.

WORDS OF TWO SYLLABLES, ACCENTED ON THE SECOND.

A-base	ad-journ	a-maze	at-tack
ab-hor	ad-mit	a-mend	at-tempt
a-bide	a-dore	a-midst	at-tire
a-bout	ad-vance	a-mong	a-vail
a-broad	a-far	a-muse	a-venge
ab-rupt	af-fair	a-noint	a-void
ab-solve	af-firm	a-part	a-wait
ab-surd	af-fright	ap-proach	a-wake
ac-cept	a-gainst	ap-prove	a-way
ac-quire	a-larm	a-rise	Be-cause
ad-dict	a-like	ar-rest	be-come
ad-dress	a-lone	a-tone	be-friend

be-fore	con-tend	de-tect	e-lope
be-gin	con-tent	de-test	em-balm
be-have	con-temn	de-vise	em-bark
be-head	con-vey	di-rect	em-broil
be-hind	cor-rect	dis-arm	e-mit
be-hold	cor-rupt	dis-band	en-chant
be-lief	cre-ate	dis-burse	en-close
be-lieve	De-bar	dis-card	en-croach
be-long	de-ceit	dis-claim	en-dear
be-neath	de-cide	dis-count	en-dorse
be-night	de-clare	dis-course	en-due
be-queath	de-coy	dis-joint	en-dure
be-set	de-crease	dis-like	en-force
be-side	de-duce	dis-lodge	en-gage
be-speak	de-duct	dis-may	en-joy
be-tween	de-fect	dis-miss	en-large
be-twixt	de-fend	dis-own	en-rage
be-wail	de-fence	dis-pel	en-rich
Ca-bal	de-fer	dis-place	en-rol
ca-nal	de-fy	dis-play	en-sue
ca-rouse	de-fine	dis-pose	en-thral
com-mence	de-form	dis-praise	en-throne
com-plain	de-fraud	dis-prove	en-tice
com-pel	de-grade	dis-robe	en-tire
com-ply	de-light	dis-sent	en-treat
com-pose	de-note	dis-turb	es-pouse
com-prise	de-part	dis-taste	e-vade
com-pute	de-pose	dis-tinct	e-vent
con-fer	de-press	dis-tort	e-vince
con-fine	de-pute	dis-trust	ex-alt
con-found	de-rive	dis-tract	ex-cel
con-fuse	de-scribe	dis-use	ex-cise
con-strain	de-sire	di-vert	ex-cite
con-sume	de-spond	di-vine	ex-claim
con-tempt	de-stroy	Ef-fect	ex-cuse

ex-empt
ex-ert
ex-ist
ex-pand
ex-pend
ex-plode
ex-pose
ex-tend
ex-tort
ex-tract
ex-treme
Fif-teen
fo-ment
fore-arm
fore-seen
fore-show
fore-stall
fore-tell
fore-told
fore-warn
for-bear
r-bid
for-get
for-give
for-sworn
four-teen
ful-fil
Ga-zette
Him-self
Im-brue
im-burse
im-merse
im-pair
im-pale
im-pend

im-plant
im-press
im-print
im-prove
in-cite
in-cur
in-dent
in-dulge
in-fect
in-fest
in-firm
in-flame
in-force
in-fringe
in-fuse
in-graft
in-grate
in-ject
in-scribe
in-slave
in-snare
in-stil
in-struct
in-sure
in-tense
in-trude
in-trust
in-verse
in-vert
in-vest
in-vite
Mis-chance
mis-count
mis-deed
mis-doubt

mis-give
mis-hap
mis-lead
mis-like
mis-name
mis-place
mis-print
mis-rule
mis-pend
mis-take
mis-trust
mo-lest
mo-rose
Neg-lect
Ob-struct
ob-tain
oc-cur
of-fence
o-mit
op-press
out-do
out-live
out-strip
Par-take
per-form
per-mit
per-spire
per-tain
per-verse
pervert
po-lite
por-tend
pre-dict
pre-judge
pre-pare

pre-vail
pre-scribe
pre-serve
pre-sūme
pre-tend
pro-mote
pro-nounce
pro-pose
pro-pound
pro-rogue
pro-tect
pro-test
pur-loin
pur-suit
Re-bate
re-buke
re-cant
re-cite
re-cline
re-course
re-duce
re-fer
re-fit
re-gain
re-joice
re-late
re-lax
re-ly
re-mark
re-mind
re-mit
re-pair
re-pass
re-pose
re-press

re-prieve	sub-orn	un-arm	un-lace
re-print	sub-scribe	un-bar	un-like
re-prove	sub-side	un-bind	un-lock
re-pulse	sub-sist	un-blest	un-made
re-strain	sub-tract	un-bolt	un-mask
re-sume	sup-pose	un-born	un-pack
re-tail	su-preme	un-bound	un-paid
re-tract	sur-mount	un-clasp	un-pin
re-trench	sur-pass	un-clean	un-ripe
re-turn	sur-vey	un-clothe	un-safe
re-vere	sur-vive	un-close	un-say
re-volve	sus-pense	un-cut	un-seen
re-ward	sus-tain	un-dress	un-sound
ro-bust	Tra-duce	un-fair	un-sung
ro-mance	trans-act	un fit	un-teach
Se-clude	tran-scend	un-fold	un-tie
se-dan	tran-scribe	un-gain	un-true
se-duce	trans-form	un-guide	un-twist
se-lect	trans-gress	un-heard	up-on
se-vere	tran-slate	un-hinge	With-al
sha-lot	trans-plant	un-hook	with-in
sub-join	trans-pose	un-horse	with-draw
sub-lime	tre-pan	un-hurt	with-out
sub-mit	Un-apt	un-just	with-stand

As-pect	Flus-ter	jus-tice	pros-trate
Bas-ket	frus-trate	Mas-ter	pub-lish
bas-tard	Glis-ter	Nos-tril	pun-ish
bush-el	glit-ter	Os-trich	Res-cue
Clus-ter	gob-let	Pas-tor	res-pite
cus-tard	gris-tle	pis-tol	Sis-ter
cus-tom	Hos-tage	pop-lar	sys-tem
Dis-taff	hon-our	prob-lem	Ves-try
dis-tant	Im-age	pros-per	ves-ture
dis-tinct	Jas-per	pros-pect	Whis-per

TABLE VIII.

EASY LESSONS OF WORDS OF ONE AND TWO SYLLABLES, BEING SELECT MORAL PRECEPTS: THE SYLLABLES ARE DIVIDED.

DUTY TO GOD.

My du-ty to-wards God is to be-lieve in him, to fear him, to love him with all my heart, with all my mind, with all my soul, with all my strength; to wor-ship him, to give him thanks, to put my whole trust in him, to call up-on him, to hon-our his ho-ly name and his word, and to serve him tru-ly all the days of my life.

OF GOD.

There is but one God, the Ma-ker of all things both in hea-ven and earth, and this God is a ho-ly, wise, just, and good Be-ing, ha-ting all man-ner of sin.

He fills hea-ven and earth with his pow-er, wis-dom, jus-tice, mer-cy, and truth, and loves all those that love and fear him, and will bless all those that love, hon-our, and o-bey their pa-rents.

As for the wick-ed, such as swear, lie, and steal, he will judge and con-demn them to shame and sor-row. Learn then be-times to know thy du-ty to God and man, and God will bless you in this world, and when you die he will take you to him-self in-to hea-ven, will clothe you in gar-ments of gold, and set a crown of gold on your head: the an-gels will re-joice to see you, and you shall be hap-py for ev-er and ev-er.

AN EXHORTATION TO VIRTUE, UNDIVIDED FOR TRIAL.

My good child, you have heard your duty to-wards God and man, and can you read and know these things without doing your duty; can you hear these marks of divine favour, and not strive with all your heart and mind, to love and serve God; to honour your parents; to mind your book; to love your church and school; and no to play with bad boys: for be you certain, tha if you seek God, he will be found of you; but if you forsake him, he will cast you off for ever.

OF PRAISE.

Praise the Lord, O my soul; and all that is within me praise his holy name.

As long as I live I will praise the Lord; I will give thanks unto God while I have my being.

Sing unto the Lord, O ye kingdoms of the earth: O sing praises unto the Lord.

Give the Lord the honour due unto his name, worship the Lord with holy worship.

In the time of trouble I will call upon the Lord, and he will hear me.

Turn thy face from my sins, and put out all my misdeeds.

WORDS OF THREE SYLLABLES, ACCENTED ON THE FIRST SYLLABLE.

TABLE IX.

Ad-mi-ral	ar-ti-choke	cap-i-tal
ad-vo-cate	Ban-ish-ment	cap-i-tol
al-co-ran	bar-ba-rism	can-dle-stick
al-der-man	bat-te-ry	can-di-date
al-ma-nac	bat-tle-ment	car-pen-ter
al-pha-bet	blun-der-buss	cat-e-chism
an-ti-dote	bra-ve-ry	cor-po-ral
ap-pe-tite	bri-be-ry	coun-sel-lor
ar-gu-ment	Cab-i-net	cru-el-ty

Di-a-dem
di-a-lect
di-a-logue
dig-ni-ty
dra-pe-ry
drow-si-ness
El-e-ment
el-e-phant
el-o-quent
en-e-my
en-ter-prise
ec-sta-cy
Fal-si-ty
fam-i-ly
fer-ven-cy
fes-ti-val
fil-thi-ness
fool-ish-ness
fur-ni-ture
Gai-e-ty
gal-le-ry
gar-ri-son
gen-er-al
gen-tle-man
grad-u-ate
gra-na-ry
grat-i-tude
gun-pow-der
Hap-pi-ness
har-bin-ger
har-mo-ny
harp-si-chord
her-e-sy
her-e-tic
her-i-tage
hos-pi-tal
hyp-o-crite
Jav-e-lin
i-dle-ness
im-ple-ment
in-fan-cy
in-fi-del
in-ju-ry
in-stru-ment
La-bour-er
lab-y-rinth
lat-i-tude
lav-en-der
leg-a-cy
lep ro-sy
lib-er-tine
lib-er-ty
lon-gi-tude
lu-na-tic
Ma-gis-trate
ma-jes-ty
main-te-nance
mar-i-ner
mar tyr-dom
mel-o-dy
mem-o-ry
mon-u-ment
moun-te-bank
Nar-ra-tive
nat-u-ral
naugh-ti-ness
neg-li-gent
nour-ish-ment
nun-ne-ry
nu-tri-ment
Ob-sta-cle
of-fi-cer
or-a-tor
or-na-ment
or-tho-dox
o-ver-sight
Pa-pa-cy
par-a-dise
par-a-graph
par-a-phrase
par-ti-cle
per-ju-ry
pi-e-ty
pin-na-cle
po-pe-ry
prin-ci-pal
prin-ci-ple
prop-er-ty
proph-e-cy
proph-e-sy
pros-e-lyte
pyr-a-mid
Quan-tity
quar-ter-ly
Read-i-ness
ref-er-ence
rem-e-dy
rep-ro-bate
roy-al-ty
Sac-ra-ment
sa-cred-ness
sac-ri-fice
sac-ri-lege
sala- ry
scan-ti-ness

scor-pi-on	tes-ta-ment	vin-e-gar
scru-ti-ny	trea-su-rer	vi-o-lence
stea-di-ness	trin-i-ty	Ul-ti-mate
sud-den-ness	tur-pen-tine	ut-ter-ance
sup-pli-ant	tur-pi-tude	Wea-ri-ness
syc-a-more	tym-pa-ny	wick-ed-ness
sym-pa-thy	Va-can-cy	wil-der-ness
syn-a-gogue	vac-u-um	work-man-ship
Tem-per-ance	vag-a-bond	Yes-ter-day
ten-der-ness	van-i-ty	youth-ful-ness
ten-den-cy	vic-to-ry	Zeal-ous-ness

TABLE X.

WORDS OF THREE SYLLABLES, ACCENTED ON THE SECOND SYLLABLE.

A-ban-don	em-bar-go	Mis-for-tune
a-base-ment	en-sam-ple	mis-ta-ken
a-bor-tive	e-ter-nal	mis-trust-ful
ad-van-tage	ên-vi-ron	Noc-tur-nal
Be-gin-ner	ex-am-ple	No-vem-ber
be-got-ten	Fa-nat-ic	Ob-serv-ance
be-hold-en	fan-tas-tic	oc-cur-rence
be-lov-ed	for-bid-den	Oc-to-ber
bra-va-do	for-sa-ken	Par-ta-ker
Ca-the-dral	Gen-teel-ly	per-form-er
co-e-qual	gre-na-do	per-fu-mer
co-hab-it	Hap-haz-ard	pre-cep-tor
con-sump-tive	hence-for-ward	pre-vent-ive
con-trib-ute	JE-HO-VAH	Re-mem-ber
con-tri-vance	il-lus-trate	re-sem-ble
De-can-ter	in-car-nate	Se-du-cer
de-mon-strate	in-cum-bent	Sep-tem-ber
de-ter-mine	in-dul-gent	spec-ta-tor
E-lec-tor	in-form er	sur-vey-or
e lope-ment	in-ter-nal	Tes-ta-tor

to bac-co	un-e-qual	un-mind-ful
tri-bu-nal	un-faith-ful	un-thank-ful
Vice-ge-rent	un-god-ly	un-time-ly
un-cov-er	un-learn-ed	un-wor-thy

TABLE XI.

WORDS OF THREE SYLLABLES, ACCENTED ON THE LAST SYLLABLE.

Ac-qui-esce	Im-ma-ture	pat-en-tee
al-a-mode	im-por-tune	Re-ad-mit
am-bus-cade	in-cor-rect	re-as-cend
ap-per-tain	in-di-rect	rec-og-nize
ap-pre-hend	in-ter-fere	rec-ol-lect
Brig-a-dier	in-ter-line	rec-om-mend
buc-a-nier	in-ter-rupt	re-com-pose
Can-non-ade	in-tro-duce	rec-on-cile
cap-a-pie	Mac-a-roon	re-con-duct
car-a-van	mag-a-zine	ref-u-gee
cir-cum-cise	mas-quer-ade	rep-ar-tee
cir-cum-vent	mis-be-come	rep-re-sent
com-pro-mise	mis-be-have	Ser-e-nade
con-tro-vert	mis-ap-ply	su-per-add
coun-ter-mand	mis-em-ploy	su-per-fine
Dev-o-tee	mort-ga-gee	su-per-sede
deb-o-nair	Na-za-rene	su-per-vise
dis-al-low	O-ver-bold	Un-der-go
dis-ap-point	o-ver-charge	un-der-neath
dis-ap-prove	o-ver-cloud	un-der-sell
dis-ap-pear	o-ver-come	un-der-stand
dis-con-cert	o-ver-drive	un-der-stood
dis-en-gage	o-ver-grown	un-der-take
dom-i-neer	o-ver-laid	un-der-took
En-ter-tain	o-ver-stock	un-der-went
ev-er-more	o-ver-thrown	un-ex-pert
Ga-zet teer	Pal-i-sade	un-gen-teel
gren-a dier	pan ta-loons	Yes-ter-night

TABLE XII.

LESSONS IN WORDS NOT EXCEEDING THREE SYLLABLES.

OF DUTY TO GOD.

You have heard and read in les-sons be-fore this, what your du-ty to God and man is; but lest you should for-get it, or not think your-self bound to do it, I re-mind you of it a-gain.

Re-mem-ber then, God ex-pects your ear-ly youth-ful days should be spent well. He gives you a strict charge, and you must o-bey him.

You must not neg-lect to serve him at church in pub-lic wor-ship; but be ve-ry rea-dy at all times when you are call-ed up-on to serve him.

You must not go to serve God by force, nor be an-gry or sor-ry when you are call-ed to church or to pray-ers; for then he will be an-gry with you, be-cause you dis-obey him and your pa-rents.

OF DUTY TO PARENTS, UNDIVIDED FOR TRIAL.

He that knows his duty to God, as he ought to do, will not fail to please and obey his parents.

Let God be the first in your thoughts when you awake, and last of all things when you go to bed; for if you thus think of God, and fear him all the day long, he will give you all the good things that this world can afford, and much more than you deserve, or even can desire.

He that loves God, will love and obey his parents, and will strive to please them in all lawful things they require of him to do.

A good boy will not pout and be sullen when he is told of a fault, but will mind what his father, mother, master, or friends say to him; and if he has any good nature or good manners, he will endeavour to amend his former faults, and to do so no more: for those children that disobey their parents seldom prosper, but often come to sorrow and some ill end.

SELECTED OUT OF THE PSALMS, AND OUT OF THE PROVERBS OF SOLOMON.

Blessed is the man that hath not walked in the counsel of the ungodly, nor stood in the way of sinners, and hath not sat in the seat of the scornful; but his delight is in the law of the Lord, and in that law will he exercise himself day and night.

As for the ungodly, it is not so with them; but they are like the chaff which the wind driveth away from the face of the earth.

The Lord knoweth the way of the righteous; but the way of the ungodly shall perish.

A wise son maketh a glad father; but a foolish son is the heaviness of his mother.

The way of a fool is right in his own eyes; but he that hearkeneth to good counsel is wise.

When a man's ways please the Lord, he maketh even his enemies to be at peace with him.

The Lord is far from the wicked; but he hears the prayers of the righteous.

The fear of the Lord is the fountain of life, to depart from the snares of death.

The fear of the Lord prolongeth days; but the years of the wicked shall be shortened.

Chasten thy son while there is hope, and let not thy soul spare for his crying; correct thy son, and he shall give thee rest; yea, he shall give delight unto thy soul.

Train up a child in the way he should go, and when he is old he will not depart from it.

The lot is cast into the lap, but the whole disposing thereof is from the Lord.

TABLE XIII.

WORDS OF FOUR SYLLABLES, ACCENTED ON THE FIRST SYLLABLE AND DIVIDED.

Ac-cep-ta-ble	fig-u-ra-tive	nec-ro-man-cy
ac-ces-sa-ry	for-mi-da-ble	Ob-sti-nate-ly
ac-cu-ra-cy	for-tu-nate-ly	or-a-to-ry
ad-ver-sa-ry	frau-du-lent-ly	Pat-ri-mo-ny
al-le-go-ry	Gen-e-ral-ly	phy-si-cal-ly
Bar-ba-rous-ly	glo-ri-ous-ly	prom-is-so-ry
blus-ter-ing-ly	gra-ci-ous-ly	pur-ga-to-ry
boun-ti-ful-ly	grad-u-al-ly	Rea-son-a-ble
Com-pe-ten-cy	Het-er-o-dox	sal-u-ta-ry
con-fi-dent-ly	hon-our-a-ble	sanc-tu-a-ry
con-ti-nen-cy	hos-pi-ta-ble	sol-i-ta-ry
con-tro-ver-sy	Im-po-ten-cy	spa-ci-ous-ly
cor-ri-gi-ble	in-ti-ma-cy	Tab-er-na-cle
Del-i-ca-cy	in-ven-to-ry	tem-po-ral-ly
dif-fi-cul-ty	Lap-i-da-ry	tran-si-to-ry
dil-i-gent-ly	lit-e-ra-ry	tes-ti-mo-ny
drom-e-da-ry	Mat-ri-mo-ny	tol-er-a-bly
Ef-fi-ca-cy	mem-o-ra-ble	Val-u-a-ble
el-e-gant-ly	mer-ce-na-ry	ve-he-ment-ly
ev-i-dent-ly	Nat-u-ral-ly	vir-tu-ous-ly
ex-em-pla-ry	nav-i-ga-ble	Whim-si-cal-ly

TABLE XIV.

WORDS OF FOUR SYLLABLES, ACCENTED ON THE SECOND SYLLABLE.

A-bom-i-nate	be-nev-o-lence	dex-ter-i-ty
ac-cel-e-rate	be-nig-ni-ty	E-gre-gi-ous
ac-com-mo-date	bi-tu-mi-nous	e-mol-u-ment
am-big-u-ous	Ca-lam-i-ty	en-thu-si-ast
am-phib-i-ous	ca-pa-ci-ty	e-quiv-o-cal
a-pol-o-gy	cap-tiv-i-ty	ex-ten-u-ate
ar-tif-i-cer	cir-cum-fer-ence	Fer-til-i-ty
au-da-ci-ous	com-mu-ni-cant	fru-gal-i-ty
au-thor-i-ty	com-mu-ni-ty	Gram-mat-i-cal
Bar-bar-i-ty	con-tem-pla-tive	Har-mo-ni-ous
be-ha-vi-our	De-bil-i-ty	hu-man-i-ty
be-nef-i-cence	de-gen-e-rate	hy-drop-i-cal

hy-poc-ri-sy	om-nip-o-tent	so-ci-e-ty
I-den-ti-ty	out-ra-ge-ous	sta-bil-i-ty
in-fir-mi-ty	Pa-thet-i-cal	Tri-en-ni-al
Le-git-i-mate	pe-cu-li-ar	Ve-ra-ci-ty
li-ti-gi-ous	pro-pri-e-tor	vi-cis-si-tude
Ma-tu-ri-ty	pro-ver-bi-al	vic-to-ri-ous
mu-nif-i-cence	Re-luc-tan-cy	vi-va-ci-ty
Na-tiv-i-ty	ri-dic-u-lous	U-biq-ui-ty
no-to-ri-ous	Sa-ga-ci-ty	un-righ-te-ous
O-be-di-ent	so-bri-e-ty	ux-o-ri-ous

TABLE XV.

WORDS OF FOUR SYLLABLES, ACCENTED ON THE THIRD SYLLABLE.

Ad-a-man-tine	For-ni-ca-tor	op-e-ra-tor
af-fi-da-vit	Hal-le-lu-jah	Pal-i-sa-do
Be-at-if-ic	hor-i-zon-tal	per-ad-ven-ture
bar-ri-ca-do	Im-i-ta-tor	pre-de-ces-sor
bas-ti-na-do	in-de-pen-dent	pro-cu-ra-tor
ben-e-fac-tor	in-dis-creet-ly	Sac-ra-men-tal
Cal-i-man-co	in-ter-mix-ture	sal-a-man-der
Car-o-li-na	Le-gis-la-ture	su-per-vi-sor
co-ex-is-tent	le-gis-la-tive	The-o-ret-ic
com-pre-hen-sive	Man-i-fes-to	Un-ad-vi-sed
cor-res-pon-dent	me-di-a-tor	un-de-fi-led
Dan-de-li-on	mem-o-ran-dum	un-der-ta-ken
de-cli-na-tor	mod-er-a-tor	un-der-val-ue
di-a-be-tes	Nav-i-ga-tor	u-ni-ver-sal
dis-ad-van-tage	non-con-form-ist	What-so-ev-er
El-e-va-tor	nu-mer-a-tor	when-so-ev-er
en-ter-tain-ment	Ob-ser-va-tor	where-so-ev-er
e-van-gel-ic	om-ni-pres-ence	who-so-ev-er
ev-er-last-ing	om-ni-pres-ent	whom-so-ev-er

WORDS OF FOUR SYLLABLES, ACCENTED ON THE LAST SYLLABLE.

An-i-mad-vert	Le-ger-de-main	Su-per-a-bound
av-oir-du-pois	Nev-er-the-less	su-per-in-duce
Car-a-bi-neer	Re-cog-ni-see	su-per-in-tend
El-e-cam-pane	re-cog-ni-sor	Ul-tra-ma-rine

TABLE XVI.

PROPER LESSONS TO EXERCISE THE YOUNG LEARNER IN ALL THE FOREGOING RULES.

PART OF THE THIRD CHAPTER OF ECCLESIASTES.

To every thing there is a season, and a time to every purpose under the heaven: a time to be born, and a time to die; a time to plant, and a time to pluck up that which is planted.

A time to kill, and a time to heal; a time to break down, and a time to build up.

A time to weep, and a time to laugh; a time to mourn, and a time to dance.

A time to cast away stones, and a time to gather stones together; a time to embrace, and a time to refrain from embracing.

A time to get, and a time to lose; a time to keep, and a time to cast away.

A time to rend, and a time to sew; a time to keep silence, and a time to speak.

A time to love, and a time to hate; a time of war, and a time of peace.

I know that whatsoever God doth, it shall be for ever: nothing can be put to it, nor any thing taken from it: and God doth it, that men should fear before him.

PART OF THE 118TH PSALM.

O give thanks unto the Lord, for he is gracious; because his mercy endureth for ever.

Let *Israel* now confess that he is gracious, and that his mercy endureth for ever.

Let the house of *Aaron* now confess, that his mercy endureth for ever.

Yea, let them now that fear the Lord confess, that his mercy endureth for ever.

I called upon the Lord in trouble; and the Lord heard me at large.

The Lord is on my side: I will not fear what man doth unto me.

The Lord taketh my part with them that help me; therefore shall I see my desire upon mine enemies.

It is better to trust in the Lord, than to put any confidence in princes.

Thou art my God, and I will thank thee: thou art my God, and I will praise thee.

O give thanks unto the Lord, for he is gracious: and his mercy endureth for ever.

PSALM THE 136TH.

1. O give thanks unto the Lord, for he is good: for his mercy endureth for ever.

2. O give thanks unto the God of all gods: for his mercy endureth for ever.

3. O thank the Lord of all lords: for his mercy endureth for ever.

4. Who only doth great wonders: for his mercy endureth for ever.

5. Who by his excellent wisdom, made the heavens: for his mercy endureth for ever.

6. Who laid out the earth above the waters for his mercy endureth for ever.

7. Who hath made great lights: for his mercy endureth for ever.

8. The sun to rule the day: for his mercy endureth for ever.

9. The moon and stars to govern the night: for his mercy endureth for ever.

10. Who smote *Egypt* with their first-born: for his mercy endureth for ever.

11. And brought out *Israel* from among them: for his mercy endureth for ever.

12. With a mighty hand and stretched-out arm: for his mercy endureth for ever.

13. Who divided the *Red Sea* in two parts: for his mercy endureth for ever.

14. And made *Israel* to go through the midst of it: for his mercy endureth for ever.

15. But as for *Pharaoh* and his host, he overthrew them in the *Red Sea:* for his mercy endureth for ever.

16. Who led his people through the wilderness: for his mercy endureth for ever.

17. Who smote great kings: for his mercy endureth for ever.

18. Yea, and slew mighty kings: for his mercy endureth for ever.

19. *Sihon*, king of the *Amorites:* for his mercy endureth for ever.

20. And *Og*, the king of *Basan:* for his mercy endureth for ever.

21. And gave away their land for an heritage: for his mercy endureth for ever.

22. Even for an heritage unto *Israel* his servant: for his mercy endureth for ever.

23. Who remembered us when we were in trouble: for his mercy endureth for ever.

24. And hath delivered us from our enemies: for his mercy endureth for ever.

25. Who giveth food to all flesh: for his mercy endureth for ever.

26. O give thanks unto the God of heaven: for his mercy endureth for ever.

27. O give thanks unto the Lord of lords: for his mercy endureth for ever

PSALM THE 139TH. OF THE MAJESTY OF GOD.

1. O Lord, thou hast searched me out, and known me; thou knowest my down-sitting and my up-rising; thou understandest my thoughts long before.

2. Thou art about my path, and about my bed; and spiest out all my ways.

3. For, lo, there is not a word in my tongue, but thou, O Lord, knowest it altogether.

4. Thou hast fashioned me behind and before; and laid thine hand upon me.

5. Such knowledge is too wonderful and excellent for me: I cannot attain unto it.

6. Whither shall I go then from thy Spirit? or whither shall I flee from thy presence?

7. If I climb up into heaven, thou art there; if I go down to hell, thou art there also.

8. If I take the wings of the morning, and remain in the uttermost parts of the sea;

9. Even there also shall thy hand lead me, and thy right hand shall hold me.

10. If I say, Peradventure the darkness shall cover me; then shall my night be turned to day.

11. Yea, the darkness is no darkness with thee, but the night is as clear as the day: the darkness and light to thee are both alike.

12. For my reins are thine: thou hast covered me in my mother's womb.

13. I will give thanks unto thee, for I am fearfully and wonderfully made: marvellous are thy works, and that my soul knoweth right well.

14. My bones are not hid from thee; though I be made secretly and fashioned beneath in the earth.

15. How dear are thy counsels unto me, O God! O how great is the sum of them!

16. If I tell them, they are more in number than the sand: when I awake, I am present with thee.

17. Try me, O God, and seek the ground of my heart: prove me, and examine my thoughts

18. Look well if there be any way of wickedness in me, and lead me in the way everlasting.

OF MORAL, RELATIVE, AND RELIGIOUS DUTIES.

1. The Proverbs of *Solomon*, the son of *David*, king of *Israel*.

2. To know wisdom and instruction, to perceive the words of understanding.

3. To receive the instruction of wisdom, justice, judgment, and equity.

4. The fear of the Lord is the beginning of knowledge; but fools despise wisdom and instruction.

5. My son, hear the instruction of thy father, and forsake not the law of thy mother; for they shall be an ornament of grace unto thy head, and chains about thy neck.

6. My son, if sinners entice thee, consent thou not.

7. If they say, Come with us, let us lay wait for blood; let us lurk privily for the innocent without cause:

8. Cast in thy lot among us; let us all have one purse:

9. My son, walk not thou in the way with them; refrain thy foot from their path: for their feet run to evil, and make haste to shed blood.

10. Enter not into the path of the wicked, and go not in the way of evil men.

11. For the wicked shall be cut off from the earth, and transgressors shall be rooted out of it.

12. But the upright shall dwell in the land, and the perfect shall remain in it.

OF ADVICE, ETC.

1. My son, attend to my words; incline thine ear unto my sayings:

2. Let them not depart from thine eyes; keep them in the midst of thy heart:

3. For they are life unto those that find them, and health to all their flesh.

4. Keep thy heart with all diligence, for out of it are the issues of life.

5. Put away from thee a froward mouth, and perverse lips put far from thee.

6. Turn not to the right hand, nor to the left; remove thy foot from evil.

7. For the ways of a man are before the eyes of the Lord; and he pondereth all his goings.

8. These six things doth the Lord hate; yea, seven are an abomination unto him:

9. A proud look, a lying tongue, and hands that shed innocent blood;

10. A heart that deviseth wicked imaginations, and feet that be swift in running to do mischief;

11. A false witness that speaketh lies, and he that soweth discord among brethren.

12. My son, keep my words, and lay up my commandments with thee.

13. Bind them upon thy fingers; write them upon the table of thine heart.

14. The fear of the Lord is a fountain of life, to depart from the snares of death.

15. There shall no evil happen to the just; but the wicked shall be filled with mischief.

16. He that is of a proud heart stirreth up strife: but he that putteth his trust in the Lord shall be made fat.

17. A virtuous woman is a crown to her husband; but she that maketh shame is as rottenness in his bones.

18. A prudent woman looks well to her household, and eats not the bread of idleness.

19. The rich and poor meet together; the Lord is the maker of them all.

20. Remember that God will bring every work into judgment, with every secret thing, whether it be good, or whether it be evil.

21. My son, if thou hast sinned, do so no more; but pray for thy former sins, and they shall be forgiven thee.

22. Flee from sin as from a serpent; for if thou comest too near to it, it will bite thee: the teeth thereof are as the teeth of a lion, to slay the souls of men.

23. All iniquity is as a two-edged sword, the wounds whereof cannot be healed.

☞ I set the figures to the verses of these last lessons, which children may very easily be taught to know, without any sensible pains to th teacher; or by turning them to table XIX. (by way of digression) they will teach one another by degrees.

N. B. If the young learner cannot read these lessons pretty perfectly, let him go over them once more; then I would advise the master or mistress to let him read some other Psalms, or in the Proverbs of Solomon, then in the first chapter of St. John the Evangelist, or any such like easy places most suitable to his capacity; for it is natural to children to like that which they can perform with ease, and have praise for: and I am persuaded many children have hated both their school and the Bible, by being put to read hard and difficult chapters too soon; and by being improperly (nay even unjustly) corrected for not performing that which they could not possibly do even were they farther advanced. What some children indeed may chance to do, is not to be accounted for; but I speak in pity to such as cannot: and to those that have the care of dull children, I speak it purely, that they may have the less trouble, and yet their end be answered much better.

WORDS OF FIVE SYLLABLES, ACCENTED ON THE SECOND.

A-BOM-I-NA-BLE	ex-tor-tion-er	ir-rev-o-ca-ble
am-bi-tious-ly	ex-trav-a-gan-cy	Las-civ-i-ous-ness
a-poth-e-ca-ry	ex-u-be-ran-cy	le-git-i-ma-cy
aux-il-i-a-ry	Har-mo-ni-ous-ly	No-to-ri-ous-ly
Com-mu-ni-ca-ble	he-red-i-ta-ry	O-ri-gi-nal-ly
con-fec-tion-er	Im-me-di-ate-ly	Pe-cu-ni-a-ry
con-fed-e-ra-cy	in-cen-di-a-ry	per-pet-u-al-ly
con-temp-tu-ous-ly	in-con-ti-nen-cy	pro-thon-o-ta-ry
con-tin-u-al-ly	in-ev-i-ta-ble	Re-pos-i-to-ry
con-trib-u-ta-ry	in-ex-o-ra-ble	Un-ne-ces-sa-ry
con-ve-ni-en-cy	in-im-i-ta-ble	un-rea-son-a-ble
Dis-cred-it-a-ble	in-nu-mer-a-ble	un-meas-ur-a-ble
Ef-fi-cien-cy	in-su-per-a-ble	un-prof-it-a-ble
e-gre-gi-ous-ly	ir-rep-a-ra-ble	un-righ-te-ous-ness
es-pe-cial-ly	ir-res-o-lute	un-sep-a-ra-ble

WORDS OF FOUR AND FIVE SYLLABLES, ACCENTED ON THE THIRD SYLLABLE.

AB-DI-CA-TION	an-ni-ver-sa-ry	com-mi-na-tion
ac-a-dem-i-cal	an-no-ta-tion	com-pe-ti-tion
ac-cep-ta-tion	ap-pa-ri-tion	com-pre-hen-si-ble
ac-cla-ma-tion	ap-pel-la-tion	com-pre-hen-sion
ac-qui-si-tion	as-si-du-i-ty	con-de-scen-sion
ad-mi-ra-tion	as-tro-lo-gi-cal	con-fla-gra-tion
ad-mo-ni-tion	as-tro-nom-i-cal	con-fu-ta-tion
ad-o-ra-tion	av-a-ri-cious	con-gre-ga-tion
ad-u-la-tion	Be-a-tif-i-cal	con-ju-ra-tion
af-fa-bil-i-ty	ben-e-dic-tion	con-se-cra-tion
af-fec-ta-tion	ben-e-fi-cial	con-so-la-tion
al-le-ga-tion	Cas-ti-ga-tion	con-stel-la-tion
al-le-gor-i-cal	cel-e-bra-tion	con-ster-na-tion
al-pha-bet-i-cal	cer-e-mo-ni-al	con-sti-tu-tion
am-bi-gu-i-ty	cir-cu-la-tion	con-sul-ta-tion
am-mu-ni-tion	cir-cum-ci-sion	con-tem-pla tion
am-pu-ta-tion	cir-cum-spec tion	con-tra-dic-tion
an-a-bap-tist	co-es-sen-tial	con-tri-bu-tion
an-i-mos-i-ty	com-bi-na-tion	con-tu-ma-cious

con-tu-me-li-ous
con-ver-sa-tion
cop-u-la-tion
cor-o-na-tion
cor-po-ra-tion
cru-ci-fix-ion
Dec-la-ma-tion
dec-la-ra-tion
ded-i-ca-tion
def-a-ma-tion
def-i-ni-tion
dem-o-crat-i-cal
dem-on-stra-tion
dep-o-si-tion
dep-ri-va-tion
dep-u-ta-tion
der-i-va-tion
des-o-la-tion
des-pe-ra-tion
dev-as-ta-tion
di-a-bol-i-cal
dis-o-be-di-ent
dis-pen-sa-tion
dis-po-si-tion
dis-so-lu-tion
dis-tri-bu-tion
div-i-na-tion
dom-i-na-tion
Ed-u-ca-tion
ef-fi-ca-cious
el-o-cu-tion
em-u-la-tion
ep-i-dem-i-cal
e-qua-nim-i-ty
es-ti-ma-tion
ex-com-mu-ni-cate
ex-e-cra-tion
ex-e-cu-tion
ex-ha-la-tion
ex-hi-bi-tion
ex-hor-ta-tion
ex-pec-ta-tion
ex-pe-di-tion
ex-pi-ra-tion
ex-pla-na-tion
ex-po-si-tion
Fer-men-ta-tion
for-ni-ca-tion
Gen-e-ra-tion
gen-e-ros-i-ty
Hab-i-ta-tion
hes-i-ta-tion
hos-pi-tal-i-ty
hyp-o-crit-i-cal
Il-le-git-i-mate
im-be-cil-i-ty
im-i-ta-tion
im-po-si-tion
in-cli-na-tion
in-cor-rup-tion
in-di-vid-u-al
in-flam-ma-tion
in-qui-si-tion
in-spi-ra-tion
in-sti-tu-tion
in-sur-rec-tion
in-ter-ces-sion
in-tro-duc-tion
in-vi-ta-tion
Ju-ris-dic-tion
lib-e-ral-i-ty
lim-i-ta-tion
Ma-gis-te-ri-al
mag-na-nim-i-ty
math-e-mat-i-cal
me-di-oc-ri-ty
med-i-ta-tion
min-is-tra-tion
mis-con-struc-tion
mod-e-ra-tion
mul-ti-pli-ci-ty
mu-ta-bil-i-ty
Nav-i-ga-tion
non-con-for-mi-ty
nu-me-ra-tion
Ob-li-ga-tion
ob-ser-va-tion
oc-cu-pa-tion
o-do-rif-e-rous
op-e-ra-tion
op-por-tu-ni-ty
op-po-si-tion
or-di-na-tion
os-ten-ta-tion
Par-ti-al-i-ty
per-pen-dic-u-lar
per-pe-tu-i-ty
per-se-cu-tion
per-spi-cu-i-ty
per-tur-ba-tion
pes-ti-len-tial
pos-si-bil-i-ty
prep-a-ra-tion
pres-er-va-tion
prin-ci-pal-i-ty
pro-cla-ma-tion
pro-di-gal-i-ty
pro-hi-bi-tion
pro-pa-ga-tion
pro-ro-ga-tion
prov-i-den-tial
prov-o-ca-tion
pub-li-ca-tion
pu-sil-lan-i-mous
pu-tre-fac-tion
Quint-es-sen-tial
Rec-ol-lec-tion
ref-or-ma-tion
re-lax-a-tion
ren-o-va-tion

rep-e-ti-tion
rep-re-hen-sion
rep-ro-ba-tion
rep-u-ta-tion
res-er-va-tion
res-o-lu-tion
res-to-ra-tion
res-ur-rec-tion
ret-ri-bu-tion
rev-e-la-tion
rev-e-ren-tial
rev-o-lu-tion
Sac-ri-le-gious
sal-u-ta-tion
sat-is-fac-tion
sep-a-ra-tion
sin-gu-lar-i-ty
sit-u-á-tion
spec-u-la-tion
suf-fo-ca-tion
su-per-fi-cial
su-per-scrip-tion
su-per-sti-tion
sup-pli-ca-tion
sup-po-si-tion
sur-rep-ti-tious
Tes-ti-mo-ni-al
tol-e-ra-tion
trans-port-a-tion
trib-u-la-tion
Val-e-dic-tion
va-ri-a-tion
ve-ge-ta-tion
ven-e-ra-tion
vin-di-ca-tion
vi-o-la-tion
Un-ad-vi-sed-ly
u-ni-form-i-ty
u-ni-ta-ri-an

WORDS OF SIX AND SEVEN SYLLABLES.

THE ACCENT IS UPON THE THIRD SYLLABLE FROM THE END, UNLESS OTHERWISE MARKED.

AB-BRE-VI-A′-TION
a-bom-i-ná-tion
ac-com-mo-dá-tion
ad-min-is-trá-tion
a″ni-mad-vér-sion
an-ni-hi-lá-tion
an-nun-ci-á-tion
ar″chi-e-pis-co-pal
a-ris-to-crat-i-cal
as-sas-si-ná-tion
as-sev-e-rá-tion
as-so-ci-á-tion
Ca″pi″tu-lá-tion
cer-e-mó-ni-ous-ly
cir-cum-lo-cú-tion
cir-cum-nav-i-gá-tion
cir-cum-vo-lú-tion
co-es-sen-ti-al-i-ty
com-mem-o-rá-tion
com-mu-ni-ca-bil-i-ty
com-mu-ni-cá-tion
con-sid-er-á-tion
con-sub-stan-ti-á-tion
con-tin-u-á-tion
cor-rob-o-rá-tion
De-lib-er-á-tion
de-li″ne-á-tion
de-nom-i-ná-tion
de-ter-mi-ná-tion
di-la″pi-dá-tion
dis-ad-van-tá-geous
dis-con-tin-u-á-tion
dis-in-gén-u-ous-ness
dis-sim-u-lá-tion
Ec-cle-si-a″sti-cal
e″di-fi-cá-tion
e-jac-u-lá-tion
en-thu-si-as-ti-cal

e-quiv-o-cá-tion
e-rad-i-cá-tion
e-vac-u-á-tion
e-vap-o-rá-tion
ex-am-i-ná-tion
ex-as″pe-rá-tion
ex-com-mu-ni-cá-tion
ex-per-i-men-tal-ly
ex-pos-tu-lá-tion
ex-ten-u-á-tion
ex-tra-ór-di-na-ry
Fa-mi-li-ar-i-ty
for-ti-fi-cá-tion
fruc-ti-fi-ca-tion
Ge-o-gráph-i-cal-ly
glo-ri-fi-cá-tion
grat-i-fi-cá-tion
He″te-ro-ge-ne-ous
his-to-ri-og-ra-pher
hu-mil-i-á-tion
Il-lib-e-ral-i-ty
i-ma-gin-a-tion
im-ma-te-ri-al-i-ty
im-mu-ta-bil-i-ty
in-com-pre-hen-si-ble
in-de-fát-i-ga-ble
in-di-vis-i-bil-i-ty
in-fal-li-bil-i-ty
in-sen-si-bil-i-ty
in-ter-pre-tá-tion
in-ter-ro-gá-tion
ir-rec-on-ci-la-ble
ir-reg-u-lar-i-ty
lat-i-tu-di-na-ri-an
Ma-the-ma-tí-cian
mis-rep-re-sen-tá-tion
mo″di-fi-cá-tion
mul-ti-pli-cá-tion
Nat-u-ral-i-zá-tion
O-be-di-én-tial
Pe-cu-li-ar-i-ty
per-pen-dic-u-lar-i-ty
plen-i-po-tén-ti-a-ry
pre-de″sti-ná-tion
pro-cras-ti-ná-tion
pro-nun-ci-á-tion
pro-pór-tion-a-ble
pu-ri-fi-cá-tion
pu-sil-lan-im-i-ty
Qua″li-fi-ca-tion
Rat-i-fi-cá-tion
re-ca-pit-u-lá-tion
re″com-men-dá-tion
rec″on-cil-i-á-tion
re-ge″ne″rá-tion
rep″re-sen-tá-tion
re-tal-i-á-tion
Sanc-ti-fi-cá-tion
sig-ni-fi-cá-tion
so″lem-ni-zá-tion
su-pe-ri-or-i-ty
Trans-fi″gu-rá-tion
tran-sub-stan-ti-á-tion
Un-cir-cum-cí-sion
un-in-ter-rup-ted-ly
u-ni-ver-sal-i-ty
Vul-ne-ra-bil-i-ty
val-e-tu-di-na-ri-an

TABLE XVII.

CONTAINS SOME USEFUL FABLES.

FABLE I. OF THE BOY THAT STOLE APPLES.

An old man found a rude boy upon one of his trees, stealing apples, and desired him to come down; but the young saucebox told him plainly he would not. Won't you, says the old man, then I will fetch you down; so he pulled up some tufts of grass, and threw at him; but this only made the youngster laugh, to think the old man should pretend to beat him out of the tree with grass only.

Well, well, says the old man, if neither words nor grass will do, I must try what virtue there is in stones: so the old man pelted him heartily with stones, which soon made the young chap hasten down from the tree, and beg the old man's pardon.

MORAL.

If good words and gentle means will not reclaim the wicked, they must be dealt with in a more severe manner.

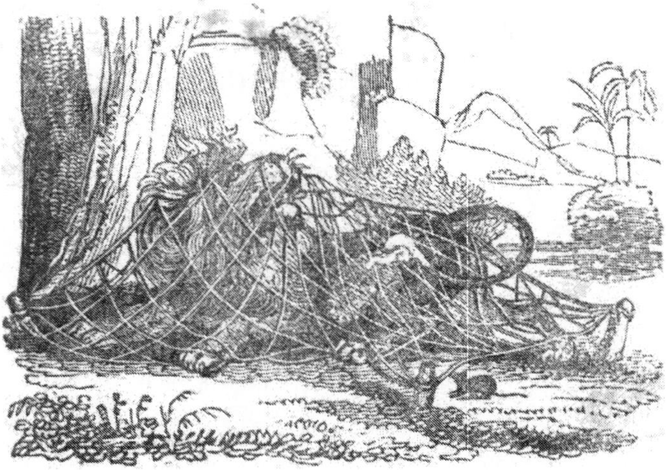

FABLE II. OF THE LION AND THE MOUSE.

THERE was a lion that was once very kind to a mouse, and saved his life from the claws of a cat. Some time after this the lion was caught in a net, in such a manner that he lay there struggling till he was half dead.

The mouse coming by at that time, was very sorry to find the lion in such a condition, and was resolved to use all the means he could to release him.

The lion, seeing the mouse so busy, thanked him for his good will, but told him, it was impossible for such a little creature as a mouse to release him out of so strong a net.

Be easy, says the mouse, what strength cannot do, art and resolution often effect; you saved my life, and gratitude obliges me to return the favour if I can.

The mouse, therefore, though not capable of breaking the net, yet set about to gnaw it asunder in several places, which, after great pains, he completed, and set the lion free.

MORAL.

Since no one knows what may befall him, nor who may be a means of serving him, it is the highest wisdom to behave kindly and civilly to all mankind.

FABLE III. OF THE PRIEST AND THE JESTER.

A MERRY jesting fellow, being half drunk, went to the house of a Romish priest, and asked him to give him a guinea. Give you a guinea! says the priest—why, surely the fellow is mad, to think I should give away my money in such a manner.

Then, said the jester, please to give me a crown, Sir. No I, indeed, says the priest; pray, begone. So I will, says the fellow, if you will give me a shilling. I will give you no shilling neither, said the priest. Why, then, said the jester, pray give me one farthing only. I will give you nothing at all, replied the priest, so begone, I say.

Pray, reverend father, be not angry, says the jester, for though I asked you for money, it was only to try you; for it is your blessing I want, and hope you will not deny it me. *That* I will give thee, my son, said the priest, with all my heart.—Come, kneel down, and receive it with humility.

I thank you, reverend father, says the arch wag; but upon second thoughts, I will not have thy cheap blessing; for I find that if it were worth but one single farthing, you would not bestow it upon me.

MORAL.

Some men are willing to part with that which is good for nothing; but cannot be prevailed upon to do a free and generous action, to help the needy or instruct the ignorant.

FABLE IV. OF THE TOWN IN DANGER OF A SIEGE.

THERE was a town in danger of being besieged, and it was consulted which was the best way to fortify and strengthen it; and many were the opinions of the town-folks concerning it.

A grave skilful mason said, there was nothing so strong nor so good as stone. A carpenter said that stone might do pretty well, but, in his opinion, good strong oak was much better.

A currier being present, said, Gentlemen, you may do as you please; but if you have a mind to have the town well fortified and secure, take my word, there is nothing like leather.

MORAL.

It is too common for men to consult their own private ends, though a whole nation suffer by it. Their own profit and emolument is all they aim at, notwithstanding they often undo themselves by betraying and undoing others.

THE SAME IN VERSE.

A town fear'd a siege, and held consultation,
Which was the best method of fortification;
A grave skilful mason gave in his opinion,
That nothing but stone could secure the dominion.
A carpenter said, though that was well spoke,
Yet 'twas better by far to defend it with oak.
A currier (wiser than both these together)
Said, Try what you please, there's nothing like leather.

MORAL.

Most men will be true to their own private ends,
Tho' false to their country, religion, and friends;
The chief thing is thought of, and that's their own profit,
Which must be secur'd whatever comes of it:
But while this self-love is a nation's undoing,
E'en they who betray it, oft sink in the ruin

TABLE XVIII.

CONTAINS SOME NATURAL ENTERTAINING STORIES.

STORY I. OF THE BOYS THAT WENT INTO THE WATER INSTEAD OF BEING AT SCHOOL OR AT HOME.

THERE were several boys that used to go into the water instead of being at school, and they sometimes staid so long after school-time, that they used to frighten their parents very much; and though they were told of it time after time, yet they would frequently go to wash themselves. One day four of them, Smith, Brown, Jones, and Robinson, took it into their heads to play the truant, and go into the water. They had not been long in before Smith was drowned. Brown's father followed him, and lashed him heartily while he was naked; and Jones and Robinson ran home half dressed, which plainly told where they had been. However, they were both sent to bed without any supper, and told very plainly, that they should be well corrected at school the next day.

By this time the news of Smith's being drowned had reached their master's ear, and he came to know the truth of it, and found Smith's father and mother in tears for the loss of him, to whom he gave very good advice, took his friendly leave, and went to see what was become of Brown, Jones, and Robinson, who all hung down their heads upon seeing their master; but more so, when their parents desired that he would correct them the next day; which he promised he would: though says he, (by the by), it is rather your duty to do it than mine, for I cannot answer for things done out of the school.

Take you care to keep your children in order at home, and depend on it I will do my duty, and keep them in awe of me at school. But, however, says he, as they have all been naughty disobedient boys, and might indeed have lost their lives, I will certainly chastise them.

HOW BROWN, JONES, AND ROBINSON WERE SERVED.

Next day Brown, Jones, and Robinson were sent to school, and in a short time were called up to their master; and he first began with Brown.—Pray, young gentleman, says he, what is the reason you go into the water, without the consent of your parents, and even when you should be at school?—I won't do so any more, says Brown.—That is nothing at all, says the master, I cannot trust you. Pray, can you swim?—No, Sir, says Brown.—Not swim, do you say! why you might have been drowned as well as Smith. Take him up, says the master. So he was taken up and well whipt.

Well, says he to Jones, can you swim?—A little, Sir, said he.—A little! says the master, why you were in more danger than Brown, and might have been drowned had you ventured much farther. Take him up, says he.

Now Robinson could swim very well, and thought, as Brown and Jones were whipt because they could not swim, that he should escape. Well, Robinson, says the master, can you swim?—Yes, Sir, says he (very boldly) any where over the river.—You can swim, you say?—Yes, Sir.—Then pray, Sir, says his master, if you can swim so well, what business had you in the water when you should have been at school? You don't want to learn to swim, you say; it is plain, then, you go in for idleness' sake. Take him up—take him up, says he. So they were all severely corrected for their disobedience and folly.

STORY II. *Life truly painted-in the natural history of Tommy and Harry, divided into three parts; by which youth may see the ways of life in general, and arm themselves against the common temptations of it, and the effects of bad company.**

PART I.

There was a gentleman in the west of England, who married a virtuous lady, but having no children for several years, they were very discontent, and foolishly upbraided each other, not duly considering that what God either gives to, or with holds from us, is always best in the end.

Some years after this they had a son, and the year following, another; the name of the elder was Henry, and the other was named Thomas, whom they loved even to an excess; for whatever Harry and Tommy's fancies stood to, they had it and as their parents never contradicted them themselves, (for

* Having been both an eye and ear witness of several circumstances of life, nearly parallel to the following fictitious narrative, I have added this to the original copy; and it has been read by several eminent clergymen, private gentlemen, and schoolmasters, who have very much approved of the same, as a proper and suitable tale by way of caution and admonition for parents as well as children. And if but one son, or daughter, or apprentice, should reap benefit thereby, so as to regulate their lives, and behave in such a manner as may conduce to their own happiness, the comfort of their parents and friends, and the good of society, I shall be very thankful, and think myself amply satisfied for my trouble.

fear they should cry) so neither would they allow any one to check them on any account, for they loved them, even to a fault, and allowed them their will and their way in every thing.*

OF THE CHARACTERS OF TOMMY AND HARRY.

Harry, indeed, was a sullen perverse boy from his cradle, and having always had his will (as was said before) he would go to school, or stay at home, just as he pleased, or else he would cry and sob at a great rate; and for fear this should make poor Harry sick, and out of order, the fond parents consent to let him do as his own fancy directed; so that he at last minds nothing but play, hates his book, and always cries when he is desired to read or go to school.

In short Harry is now seven years of age, and can scarcely read a verse in the Bible, or a sentence in a common book; and now his over-fond parents begin to see their own folly, and are afraid to tell each other what they think concerning him.

As for Tommy, he was quite of another temper; for though he would now and then cry, and be naughty, yet he minded what his parents said to him; he loved his book and his school, and was so good-natured, pleasant, and mannerly, that all his friends took notice of him; the neighbours loved him, and every body praised him, because he was a sober, good-natured child, and very dutiful and obliging.

OF TOMMY AND HARRY'S BEHAVIOUR.

Harry, indeed, minds nothing but idling and playing about the streets with any sort of boys, and it is now very difficult to get him to school, nor can his parents prevail upon him, by any means, to mind his learning; and, therefore, it is agreed upon to put them both to some good boarding-school: and accordingly their father provided a master, one that bore an extraordinary character for his ability, care, and sobriety, which it appeared he deserved, by the improvement that Tommy made under him in the several branches of learning, to the satisfaction of his parents.

* Though this tale is now divided into lessons (by desire of several schoolmasters), in order to make it more useful, easy, and agreeable to children; yet it is the very same as in other editions, and may be read from the beginning to the end as one continued story.

As for Harry, though he behaved pretty well for some time, yet he showed his sullen, perverse temper, and made very little improvement in his learning; for he went on in his old way, and played only with rude wicked boys like himself, who, in a short time, learned him to swear and lie, and some say, to steal; and he was very often angry, and would quarrel with his brother Tommy because he would not play with them; but Tommy told him plainly he would never play at all, rather than play with such wicked swearing boys, for, says he, they will be your ruin, brother Harry; and you know it grieves poor papa and mamma. I don't care for that, says naughty Harry.—O fie! fie! brother Harry, says Tommy, how often have you been told, that *don't care* has brought many a one to an ill end! I don't care for that neither, says the little churl: and thus he went on (as you will soon hear) till *don't care* was his ruin at last.

PART II.

A FARTHER ACCOUNT OF THE LIFE OF TOMMY AND HARRY.

TOMMY and Harry being now grown up, they are taken from school, and it begins to be high time to think how they may live in the world without their parents.

Tommy, indeed, was a very good boy; he always counted learning a fine thing; and he still takes delight in it, and pursues it: but Harry continues much the same; for he is nearly fourteen years of age, and is no other than a wicked boy, and a great overgrown dunce.

He hates his brother Tommy, because he loves his book, and is spoken well of; but Tommy pities him, and gives him always good advice, but to no purpose, for he is bent upon being bad, and bad it seems he will be; nor can his father, mother, or friends make him better at present. In short, Tommy is now the joy and comfort of his parents, but Harry grieves them so much, that they know not as yet how to proceed with him; nor is there now but one way left by which they have any hopes to serve him, and make them all happy.

The gentleman had a brother, (a reputable tradesman in London), and it was proposed to put Harry to his uncle. The uncle agrees to the proposal; Harry also seems well pleased at it: and now his parents promise themselves great comfort in their own and his future happiness.

OF HARRY'S BEHAVIOUR AT HIS UNCLE'S.

When Harry had been about a year in London, Tommy went to see him, and behaved so well the time he was there, that a merchant, who used to visit nis uncle, took a great fancy to him, and barely for his learning and good behaviour, took him apprentice.

Harry went on pretty well for two years: he would indeed now and then show his sullen preverse temper, but his uncle and aunt winked at his follies, hid his faults, and forgave him, for the sake of his worthy parents.

Now comes the trial for Tommy and Harry: their mother is taken very ill, and is confined to her bed: she often speaks of Tommy and Harry, but seems to have Harry most at heart, for fear he should not do well.

Not long after this, a letter comes to acquaint them of the death of their mother; and now Harry's uncle talks to him again very sedately and tenderly.

You see, Harry, says he, that you have lost your best friend; but, notwithstanding, if you behave soberly, mind your business, keep good company and good hours, I will take care of you, will be a good friend to you, and make you a man in the world.

OF HARRY'S BEHAVIOUR AFTER HIS MOTHER'S DEATH.

Harry, upon the news of his mother's death, seemed very much concerned (for he knew she was a very tender mother), and promised very fairly to mend his way of life, and be sober; but that which had a greater effect upon Harry, was the pretty way in which his brother Tommy addressed him. He talked in so mild and manly a manner to his brother Harry, and gave him such good advice, that he got the good will of his uncle and aunt, and surprised all that heard him.

Harry, after this, went on pretty well for some months, and then gets into his old way again. He has now quite forgotten the death of his mother; and, in short, has taken up with such idle wicked companions as are bent only upon mischief, and are never sorry but when they do good: they give him bad advice, and tell him, when his father is dead he will have a good fortune; and, say they, I would not be checked by my uncle, nor all the uncles in the world. I will not, says the wicked unguarded boy, for as soon as my father dies, I'll go away. That's right, say they, you are a fool if you don't: I will, I will, says he.

PART III.

OF THE HAPPY LIFE OF TOMMY, AND THE WRETCHED END OF HARRY.

THE FOLLY OF RECEIVING BAD ADVICE.

HARRY, by the bad counsel of others, still goes on in wickedness, to such a height, that his uncle is obliged to send word to his father, that he cannot possibly keep him much longer. The death of their mother, and the bad course of Harry's life, had such an effect upon the poor old gentleman, that he soon after fell ill and died.

He left Tommy, indeed, the chief part of his fortune; and though Harry did not deserve a shilling, yet so tender was he, that he left him five hundred pounds, hoping still, that through the care of his uncle, and his own future conduct, he might be happy.

Harry being now of age, and having received his fortune, instead of minding his uncle and brother, continues to follow bad company; and now, having money, he is persuaded, (and foolishly persuades himself), that he can live better from his uncle than with him, and therefore he resolves, that his uncle's and brother's advice shall never do him good, for he never comes near them.

In short, Harry's delight is only in his old wicked acquaintance; and he has, besides these, some new rakes, that wish him joy in his fortune, and he takes it as a very great mark of their favour; and is foolish enough to treat them, because they rail at his uncle and brother, and tell him that his father was an old scoundrel for leaving him no more; all which the fool hears with a smile, swears it is true, and tells these vultures, that they are the best friends he has in the world, notwithstanding he has already spent the greatest part of his fortune upon them.

OF BAD HABITS.

Here we may plainly see what a sad thing it is to youth, to bend their minds so much to pleasure and pastime.

Harry cannot now go to a play or concert, and when it is over, return home soberly as he used to do. No, no, he must after that go to the tavern, or to some private wicked place or other, with a set of vile companions.

In short, he is now become a perfect owl, for you seldom see him in the day-time; and, when you do, he blinks like an owl: nor can you find him at night, but by chance; but this you may be sure of, that he is at some house of ill fame; for drinking, swearing, lying, gaming, sitting up all night, &c. are now his common practices.

Now, while foolish wicked Harry is thus wasting his time, spending his money, and destroying his reputation, Tommy is improving his fortune and his mind; for his time being now out, his master loves him so well, that he not only takes him into partnership, but in a short time recommends him to a virtuous wife, with whom he had a very handsome fortune, besides a thousand pounds which his master gave him; and we hear, that his master since that has left all the trade to him; so that he is now become a great man.

OF BROTHERLY LOVE.

One thing must not be omitted, as a great mark of the brotherly love of Tommy, and that is, that, though he is now so prosperous, and his brother Harry so debased by his folly, yet, as he found Harry would not come near him, he resolved (if possible) to find him out, and talk to him once more concerning his unhappy life; for who knows, says he, but the respect I show to my brother may be taken so kindly, that it may be one great step to reform him. Tommy, therefore, takes a friend with him, for fear of danger, and, after a long hunt, found him at one of his old houses.

Tommy, at first sight, did not know Harry, he looked so sottish, and so shabby; nor did Harry immediately know his brother Tommy, because his dress, carriage, and deportment, were such as Harry and his companions had for a long time been strangers to.

However, they soon knew one another by the tone of voice: and, indeed, Harry had so much good manners left, as to tell Tommy, that he took it very kind he should pay such a regard to him; a respect, says he, (before his companions), that I am not worthy of.

Now one would think, by such an expression as this, that Harry was really sensible of his faults; and, in short, his brother was surprised to hear such a sentence from him, and thought with himself, that he should now certainly succeed in being a means to save him from the very brink of ruin.

Indeed the place was quite improper for good advice, much less to talk over family affairs; therefore, after Tommy had submitted to be agreeable to such base company for an hour or two, he persuaded his brother Harry to go to a tavern to spend an hour with him and his friend, to which Harry consented.

TOMMY AND HARRY'S CONVERSATION.

Tommy, being now in a proper place, begins to talk to Harry very seriously, but yet so tenderly and so mildly, that he never once upbraided him, only desired him for God's sake, and the credit of his family, to change his way of life, for, says he, the company you keep will certainly be your ruin. I don't care for that, says the hardened wretch.

O brother Harry, says Tommy, I have now no hopes of you : yet as God has prospered me, it is my duty to serve you as a brother; I will therefore make you an offer, before this gentleman, which, if you accept of it, must certainly be for your good; but, if you refuse it, I fear you will repent it when too late.

The thing is this : if you can but be so much master of yourself as to abandon such company as we have now found you with, and will behave in a sober manner, you shall live with me : I will learn you my business, and you shall partake of the profits of it; in short, you shall want for nothing.

Here was love indeed! who could have thought Harry so mad, and so stupid as not to accept so kind an offer? or who could expect but that he would have embraced his brother with tears of love and gratitude? Instead of this he rose up in a great passion, and swore like a hector, bent his fist at his brother, and told him that he kept better company than he did every day of his life, and that he never would live such a hum-drum life as he lived; then flew to the door, never took leave of the gentleman, nor his brother, but ran to his companions, and told all that had passed; they clap their hands and receive him with shouts of applause, call for a fresh bottle, and spend the main part of the night in drinking and carousing.

OF HARRY'S DOWNFALL.

Thus Harry goes on till he has not only spent all his money, but has also lost all his credit, reputation, and friends; and having been so long used to such a lavishing profligate way of life, money he still must have to support his extravagance and folly; and yet, so great is the pride of his heart, that, rather than accept of his brother Tommy's kind invitation to live with him, and be happy, he now takes up with unlawful methods, and associates with none but gamblers, shop-lifters, and street-robbers: and, one night having been with some of the rakes and bloods of the town, they committed a murder and a robbery; but, being closely pursued, Harry with four more of the gang, were taken and carried before a magistrate, who ordered them to Newgate.

Harry, however, with two others made their escape, and went over sea in triumph, and would often laugh at the misfortune of those two that were left behind, and thought themselves now very secure; but even *thither* divine vengeance followed them; for a storm arose, and drove the ship against a rock on the coast of Barbary, and, it being very dark, many of the crew perished, besides Harry's two unhappy companions.

OF HARRY'S LATE REPENTANCE AND DEATH.

Harry, indeed, was, by the violence of the waves, cast upon the shore, but in the morning he was presented with a shocking scene—a raging sea on one side, and a wild desolate place on the other; and, having not the least hopes of ever escaping, we may easily guess how he talks to himself.—O, says he, that I had been more obedient to my parents, and more grateful to my friends! O that I could now make all wicked youths sensible of my sorrow, and their own folly! how would I press upon them to avoid all manner of ill company, to hearken to the instruction of their friends, and pursue the paths of virtue.—Wicked wretch, that I am!—God, be merciful to me a sinner!

Thus he went on, often thinking upon his old words, *don't care,* but too late; for, after roving about, and bemoaning his unhappy fate, till he was almost starved to death, he at last (we hear) became a prey to wild beasts, which God suffered to tear him to pieces, as the just reward of his disobedience and mispent life.—Thus, you see, that as Harry followed nothing but vice, he lived a wretched life, and died a miserable death; but Tommy was always a pattern of virtue and goodness, and still lives happy.

THE APPLICATION.

Learn then betimes, O youth, to know your duty to God, your parents, and mankind in general, and take care not only to know, but to do it; and let the examples of Harry and Tommy be always so before you, that you may escape the just judgment of the one, and enjoy equal peace and prosperity with the other.

I shall conclude this story with the advice that king David (a little before his death) gave to his son Solomon, which, if you follow, you cannot fail to be happy.

"And thou, Solomon, my son, know thou the God of thy father, and serve him with a perfect heart, and with a willing mind; for the Lord searcheth all hearts, and understandeth all the imaginations of the thoughts: If thou seek him, he will be found of thee; but if thou forsake him, he will cast thee off for ever." 1 *Chron.* xxviii. 9.

TABLE XIX.

OF FIGURES OR NUMBERS.

N. B. It is supposed that the youth by this time knows something of numbers or figures, so as to tell what chapter he reads in, or what verse he is at; lest he should not know them at present, I have here inserted a very useful table, which every master and mistress may teach their scholars by degrees with ease.

One	1	I	Forty	40	XL
Two	2	II	Forty-five	45	XLV
Three	3	III	Fifty	50	L
Four	4	IV	Fifty-five	55	LV
Five	5	V	Sixty	60	LX
Six	6	VI	Sixty-five	65	LXV
Seven	7	VII	Seventy	70	LXX
Eight	8	VIII	Seventy-five	75	LXXV
Nine	9	IX	Eighty	80	LXXX
Ten	10	X	Eighty-five	85	LXXXV
Eleven	11	XI	Ninety	90	XC
Twelve	12	XII	Ninety-five	95	XCV
Thirteen	13	XIII	One hundred	100	C
Fourteen	14	XIV	Two hundred	200	CC
Fifteen	15	XV	Three hundred	300	CCC
Sixteen	16	XVI	Four hundred	400	CCCC
Seventeen	17	XVII	Five hundred	500	D
Eighteen	18	XVIII	Six hundred	600	DC
Nineteen	19	XIX	Seven hundred	700	DCC
Twenty	20	XX	Eight hundred	800	DCCC
Twenty-five	25	XXV	Nine hundred	900	DCCCC
Thirty	30	XXX	One thousand	1000	M
Thirty-five	35	XXXV	Two thousand	2000	MM

OTHER NUMBERS, FOR INSTRUCTION.

27	Twenty-seven	810	Eight hundred and ten.
62	Sixty-two	1600	One thousand six hundred.
112	One hundred and twelve.	1836	One thousand eight hundred and thirty-six, MDCCCXXXVI.
704	Seven hundred and four.		

TABLE XX.

Of contractions of such things as are necessary to be understood, in which whole words and sentences are known by certain letters only.

A. B. or *B. A.* bachelor of arts
Abp. archbishop
Acct. accompt
A. D. in the year of our Lord
A. M. ante meridiem, forenoon
M. A. master of arts
A. P. G. professor of astronomy in Gresham college
Bart. baronet
B. C. before Christ
B. D. bachelor of divinity
B. L. bachelor of laws
Bp. bishop
Capt. captain
Ch. or *chap.* chapter
Col. colonel
Cr. creditor
C. P. S. keeper of the privy seal
C. S. keeper of the seal
Cwt. a hundred weight
D. D. doctor in divinity
Dec. December
Deut. Deuteronomy
Do. or *ditto*, the same
Dr. doctor, and debtor
E. east
Eccles. Ecclesiasticus
Ep. epistle
Eph. Ephesians
Esq. esquire
Ex. Exodus, or example
Exon. Exeter
Exr. executor
Feb. February
F. R. S. fellow of the royal society
Gal. Galatians
Gen. Genesis, and general
Gent. gentleman
G. R. Gulielmus Rex, William the king
Heb. Hebrews
H. M. S. his majesty's ship
J. H. S. Jesus, Saviour of men
K. B. knight of the Bath
K. C. knight of the Crescent
Knt. knight
L. D. Lady-day
Ldp. lordship
Lev. Leviticus
Lieut. lieutenant
L. L. D. doctor of laws
M. marquess
M. D. doctor of physic
Messrs. gentlemen
M. P. member of parliament
Mr. master
Mrs. mistress
MS. manuscript
MSS. manuscripts
N. north, and note
N. B. nota bene, mark well
No. number
Nov. November
Obt. obedient
Oct. October
Oz. ounce
Per cent. by the hundred
Philom. a lover of mathematics
P. M. G. professor of music Gresham college
P. M. post meridiem, afternoon
P. S. postscript
Q. question
Qy. query
Regr. register
Rev. Revelations and reverend
Rt. hon. right honourable
Rt. wpful. right worshipful
S. or *St.* saint
Sec. secretary
Servt. servant
Xmas. Christmas
Xn. Christian
Xphr. Christopher

Other contractions made use of in printing or writing

d. denarium, a penny
e. g. or *v. g.* as for example
i. e. id est, that is
q. d. as if he should say
q. l. as much as you please
s. a sufficient quantity
s. solidus, a shilling
v. verse
vide, see
viz. videlicit, that is to say
& and
&c. and so forth

TABLE XXI.

A COLLECTION OF WORDS NEARLY ALIKE IN SOUND, BUT DIFFERENT IN SPELLING AND SIGNIFICATION.

N. B.—I think it very necessary that all such as can read pretty well, should now learn to know the meaning of words; for without this, the spelling part is of little signification; therefore if the young scholar were set eight or ten words of this table every night, or but two or three times a week, to spell, and tell the meaning of (according to his capacity) it would certainly be of great service.

And though I would be thought to have the highest regard for the word of God, yet I would advise all masters and mistresses to set their scholars a collection of these words (or of those in the latter part of this book) at their breakings up, rather than to write out, or get by heart, a long chapter, which they seldom mind to perform till within a day or two of returning to school again, and then sloven over their writing and spoil their hand; and, after being corrected for this, or not getting the heavy task by heart, they begin in their early days to hate the Bible, and hold the best of books in contempt; which, if read at proper times, and with due attention, would have a quite different effect upon their minds.

ABEL, a man's name
Able, strong, skilful
Accept, to receive kind- [ly
Except, to exclude
Access, an approach
Excess, a superfluity
Accidence, grammar
Accidents, chances
Accompt, a computation
Account, consideration
Acts, deeds
Axe, a woodman's tool
Adds, joins
Adze, a cooper's tool
Affect, to move or imitate
Effect, to accomplish
Ah! an interjection, denoting compassion and complaint
Awe, reverential fear
Ail, to be sick
Ale, fermented malt [liquor
Air, an element
Are, plural of *is*
E'er, ever
Ere, before
Heir, he who inherits
Alder, a tree
Elder, having more years
Alehoof, an herb

Aloof, at a distance
All, the whole
Awl, a cobbler's tool
Aloud, with a strong [voice
Allow'd, granted
Altar, a place for sacrifice
Alter, to change
An, one, some, any
Ann, a woman's name
Anchor, belonging to a ship
Anker, a measure of 9 [gallons
Ant, the name of an insect
Aunt, a parent's sister
Arc, part of a circle
Ark, a chest or ship
Arrant, notorious
Errand, a message
Errant, wandering
Ascent, an acclivity
Assent, consent
Assistance, help, support
Assistants, helpers
Attendance, waiting, serving
Attendants, servants
Augur, a tool for boring holes
Augur, a soothsayer

Baal, a Canaanitish idol
Ball, a dance, a globe
Bawl, to speak loud
Bacon, preserved swine's flesh
Baken, participle of [bake
Bail, surety
Bale, pack of goods
Bait, an allurement, a refreshment
Bate, to diminish
Baize, coarse woollen cloth
Bays, an honorary gar- [land
Base, vile
Bass, a term in music
Bald, without hair
Bawl'd, cried vehe- [mently
Ballad, a song
Ballet, an historical dance
Ballot, voting
Balm, an odoriferous [plant
Barm, yest
Barbara, a woman's name
Barbary, a country
Barberry, a small rich fruit
Bare, naked, poor
Bear, a rough shaggy [animal
Baron, a lord

Barren, unfruitful
Be, to exist
Bee, an insect that gathers honey
Bean, a kind of pulse
Been, participle of *to be*
Beach, the sea-coast or shore
Beech, a tree so called
Beau, a fop
Bo! a word of terror
Bow, an instrument
Beer, malt drink
Bier, a carriage for the dead [vessel
Bell, a sounding metal
Belle, a gay lady
Berry, a small fruit
Bury, to inter
Bile, gall, an angry swelling [heat
Boil, to bubble up with
Blew, did blow
Blue, a colour
Boar, the male of swine
Bore, to pierce a hole
Bor'd, did bore
Board, a thin plank
Boarder, one who boards [boundary
Border, an edge or
Boat, a small sailing vessel
Bought, purchased
Bodice, woman's stays
Bodies, persons or
Bold, daring [things
Bowl'd, did bowl
Bomb, a mortar shot
Boom, a bar of wood
Book, a volume for reading
Buck, the male of deer
Born, brought into life
Borne, supported [limit
Bourn, a boundary or
Burn, a rivulet, a scald
Borough, a corporate town
Burrow, a rabbit hole
Bough, a branch [ence
Bow, an act of rever-
Boy, a male child
Buoy, to bear up

Buy, to purchase
By, near
Brace, to tighten
Braze, to solder with
Braid, a knot [brass
Bray'd, pounded
Brake, a thicket of brambles [violence
Break, to shatter by
Breach, infringement, a gap
Breech, the hind part
Breaches, plural of *breach* [dress
Breeches, part of man's
Bread, food made of ground corn
Bred, brought up
Breast, a part of the body [France
Brest, a sea-port in
Brews, makes malt liquor [tusion
Bruise, a hurt or con-
Bridal, a nuptial feast
Bridle, a check, a restraint [liberty
Britain, THE land of
Briton, a native of Britain [place
Caen, the name of a
Cane, a walking-stick
Calais, a sea-port in France [cup
Chalice, the communion
Calendar, an almanac
Calender, to dress cloth
Call, to name, to summon [wig
Caul, part of a cap or
Candid, ingenuous
Candy'd, conserved
Cannon, a great gun
Canon, an ecclesiastical law [grains
Carat, a weight of 4
Carrot, an esculent root
Catch, to lay hold of
Ketch, a small ship
Cattle, beasts of pasture
Kettle, a boiler
Ceiling, the inner roof
Sealing, fixing with a seal

Celery, a salad herb
Salary, a settled hire
Cell, a small close room
Sell, to dispose of
Cellar, a vault
Seller, one who sells
Censer, an incense pan
Censor, a Roman magistrate
Censure, blame
Cent. a hundred
Scent, a smell
Sent, despatched
Centaury, an herb
Century, 100 years
Sentry, a guard
Cere, to smear with wax
Sear, to burn with an
Seer, a prophet [iron
Cession, yielding, quitting [justices
Session, an assembly of
Chagrin, vexation
Shagreen, skin of the dog fish
Chair, a moveable seat
Char, household day-
Chas'd, pursued [work
Chaste, undefiled
Chews, masticate
Choose, to cull or pick
Chouse, to cheat
Choir, a set of singers
Quire, 24 sheets of paper
Choler, wrath [neck
Collar, a ring for the
Chord, the line of a
Cord, a rope, [circle
Chronical, inveterate
Chronicle, a register
Cinque, five [water
Sink, a drain for foul
Scion, a young shoot
Sion, a mount
Cit, a citizen
Sit, to be seated
Cite, to summon [ing
Sight, the sense of see-
Site, situation
Civil, peaceable, compliant [place
Seville, the name of a
Clause, an article of a deed

Claws, talons
Cleaver, a butcher's tool
Clever, ingenious
Climb, to clamber up
Clime, climate
Close, to shut
Clothes, apparel
Coarse, homely
Course, a race-ground
Coat, a garment [bed
Cot, a hut, a swinging
Quote, to cite a passage
Coffer, a chest [coughs
Cougher, one who
Coffin, a chest for the dead [tion
Coughing, expectora-
Coin, stamped money
Kine, plural of *cow*
Coin'd, stamped [ging
Kind, affectionate, obli-
Coit, a circular piece of iron, used in the game of coits
Kite, a bird of prey
Collation, bestowing a gift
Collation, a repast
Comet, a blazing star
Commit, to intrust
Coming, approaching
Cumin, a plant
Common, public
Commune, to converse
Complement, a full number
Compliment, flattery
Concent, harmony
Consent, acquiescence
Concert, a musical entertainment
Consort, a spouse
Condemn, to find guilty
Contemn, to despise
Confidence, honest boldness [friends
Confidants, trusty
Cool'd, made less warm
Could, was able to
Correspondence, intercourse
Correspondents, those who correspond by letters

Council, an assembly
Counsel, advice
Courier, a messenger
Currier, a dresser of leather
Cousin, a relation
Cozen, to cheat
Creak, to make a noise
Creek, a small bay
Crick, a stiffness in the neck
Crewel, a ball of yarn
Cruel, inhuman
Crews, ships' companies
Cruise, to sail
Currant, a berry
Current, passable
Cygnet, a young swan
Signet, a seal
Cymbal, a drum
Symbol, a sign
Cyprus, an island, a kind of silky gauze
Cypress, a tree [brutes
Dam, a mother of
Damn, to condemn
Dane, a native of Denmark
Deign, to vouchsafe
Day, a part of time
Dey, a Moorish prince
Dear, valuable, beloved
Deer, a forest animal
Debtor, one that oweth
Deter, to frighten
Decease, a death
Disease, a distemper
Disseize, to dispossess
Defer, to delay
Differ, to disagree
Deference, respect
Difference, disagreement
Dependence, reliance
Dependents, hangers-on
Descent, a declivity
Dissent, to differ in opinion
Devices, inventions
Devises, contrives
Devizes, a borough in Wiltshire
Dew, a moisture
Due, owing

Dier, one who dies
Dire, dreadful [cloth
Disperse, to scatter
Disburse, to lay out
Divers, several
Diverse, different
Doe, a female deer or rabbit
Dough, unbaked paste
Doer, a performer
Door, entrance to a house
Does, plural of *doe*
Doze, a slumber
Dollar, a Spanish coin
Dolor, grief
Dome, an arched roof
Doom, a judgment
Done, performed
Dun, a colour [*do*
Dost, second person of
Dust, dry earth
Draft, a bill or cheque
Draught, quantity drank [pent
Dragon, a winged ser-
Dragoon, a horse soldier
Ear, the organ of hearing [months
Year, twelve calendar
Earn, to gain by labour
Yearn, to melt in pity
Easter, Christ's resurrection [name
Esther, a woman's
Eaten, swallowed
Eton, a town in Bucks.
Emerge, to rise from
Immerge, to plunge in-
Eminent, celebrated [to
Imminent, threatening
Emit, to send forth
Emmet, an ant
Enter, to go into
Inter, to bury [ister
Envoy, a public min-
Envy, ill-will [out
Eruption, a breaking
Irruption, an invasion
Ewe, a female sheep
Yew, a tree so called
You, yourself
Ewer, a water jug
Use, custom, use

Your, belonging to you
Exercise, to employ
Exorcise, to cast out de-
Extant, in being [vils
Extent, dimension
Eye, the organ of sight
I, myself
Fain, desirous
Fane, a weathercock
Feign, to dissemble
Faint, languid, weary
Feint, a pretence
Fair, beautiful
Fare, food, hire [pigs
Farrow, to bring forth
Furrow, a trench
Favour, kindness [ed
Fever, a disease so call-
Feat, exploit
Feet, plural of *foot*
Felon, a hot sore, a whitlow
Felon, a criminal
File, a smith's tool
Foil, to overcome
Fillip, a jerk with the finger
Philip, a man's name
Fir, a deal tree.
Fur, the soft hair of animals [insect
Flea, a troublesome
Flee, to fly to avoid
Flay, to strip off the skin
Flew, pret. of to *fly*
Flue, soft down, a chimney
Flour, ground corn
Flower, a blossom
Foremast, the head-mast of a ship
Foremost, first in place
Forth, abroad [bers
Fourth, a term in num-
Foul, filthy
Fowl, a bird
Frays, quarrels
Phrase, a sentence
Frances, a woman's name
Francis, a man's name
Freeze, to congeal
Frieze, a sort of cloth

Furs, the plural of *fur*
Furze, a prickly bush
Gabelle, a tax on salt
Gable, part of a building [ing
Gait, manner of walk-
Gate, a door-way
Gall, bile
Gaul, a Frenchman
Gallon, a measure of 4 quarts
Galloon, narrow riband
Genius, mental power
Genus, a kind
Gesture, action
Jester, a joker [gold
Gild, to adorn with
Guild, a corporation
Gilt, adorned with gold
Guilt, sin [egg
Glaire, the white of an
Glare, great brightness
Glutinous, sticky
Gluttonous, greedy
Gnat, a stinging fly
Nat, contraction of *Nathaniel*
Grate, a fire-place
Great, large, noble, eminent
Grater, a perforated file
Greater, larger, more noble
Grease, soft fat
Greece, a country
Groan, a deep sigh
Grown, increased
Groat, 4 pence [sure
Grot, a cave of plea-
Guess'd, conjectured
Guest, a visitor [salute
Hail, frozen rain, to
Hale, to drag by force
Hair, covering of the head [chase
Hare, an animal of
Hall, a great room
Haul, to pull
Hallow, to consecrate
Hollow, empty
Harass, to tire and fatigue [estry
Arras, hangings of tap-
Harsh, severe

Hash, minced meat [roe
Hart, the male of the
Heart, the seat of life
Haven, an harbour
Heaven, God's throne
Heal, to cure [the foot
Heel, the hind part of
He'll, he will
Hear, hearken
Here, in this place
Heard, did hear
Herd, a drove of cattle
Height, space upwards
Hight, called, named
Hew, to chop
Hue, colour
Hugh, a man's name
Hie, to make haste
High, lofty
Higher, more high
Hire, wages
Ire, great anger, wrath
Him, that man
Hymn, a godly song
Hoar, frozen dew
Whore, a lewd woman
Hoarse, having a rough voice [animal
Horse, a well-known
Hole, a cavity [thing
Whole, the total of a
Holy, pious, sacred
Wholly, entirely
Hoop, a band for a tub
Whoop, to shout
Hour, 60 minutes
Our, relating to us
Idle, lazy, worthless
Idol, an image
Idyl, a pastoral poem
Ile, part of a church
Isle, an island
Impostor, a cheat
Imposture, fraud
In, within
Inn, a public-house
Incite, to stir up
Insight, knowledge
Indict, to impeach
Indite, to compose [ous
Ingenious, witty, curi-
Ingenuous, candid, honest [ness
Innocence, harmless-

Innocents, babes
Intense, excessive
Intents, purposes
Jam, a conserve of fruit
Jamb, the post of a door
Jewry, Judea
Jury, persons sworn on trials
Joust, a mock fight
Just, upright
Kill, to murder
Kiln, a stove to dry malt, or burn lime
Knap, a protuberance, to bite [down
Nap, a short sleep,
Knave, a petty rascal
Nave, part of a wheel
Knead, to work dough
Need, necessity [knee
Kneel, to rest on the
Neal, to temper with heat [bell
Knell, the sound of a
Nell, corruption of Eleanor
Knew, did know
New, not worn or used
Knight, a title of honour [darkness
Night, the time of
Knit, to work stockings
Nit, the egg of a louse
Knot, a tied part, a knob [nial
Not, a particle of de-
Know, to understand
No, nay, not so
Knows, doth know
Nose, the organ of smell [want
Lacks, doth lack or
Lax, loose
Lade, to load
Laid, placed
Lain, did lie
Lane, a narrow road
Lair, the bed of a wild beast, a shelter
Layer, a stratum [over
Laps, licks up, folds
Lapse, a slip or oversight [man language
Latin, the ancient Ro-
Latten, iron tinned over
Lattice, a window
Lettice, a woman's name
Lettuce, a salad plant
Lead, a heavy metal
Led, conducted [tree
Leaf, the foliage of a
Lief, willingly
Leak, to run in or out
Leek, a kind of onion
Leaper, a jumper
Leper, a leprous person
Lear, a man's name
Leer, an arch look
Least, smallest [fear of
Lest, in case that, for
Lessen, to make less
Lesson, a task in reading
Lesser, smaller [a lease
Lessor, one who grants
Levee, attendance at court [or men
Levy, to raise money
Liar, one who tells lies
Lier, one who rests
Lyre, a musical instrument
Lickerish, delicate, nice
Licorice, a sweet root
Lieu, instead of
Loo, a game at cards
Lighter, more light, a boat [time
Loiter, to idle away
Limb, a leg or an arm
Limn, to paint a face
Limber, pliant [painter
Limner, a portrait
Line, a string
Loin, the waist, a joint
Links, joins together
Lynx, a sharp-sighted
Lo! behold [animal
Low, mean, humble
Load, a burden
Low'd, did low
Loam, rich earth
Loom, a weaver's frame
Loan, any thing lent
Lone, solitary
Loch, a lake [cure
Lock, to fasten or se-
Loth, unwilling
Loath, to nauseate
Loose, to slacken
Lose, to suffer loss
Lore, learning
Lower, to lessen or bring low
Made, finished
Maid, a virgin
Mail, armour, a post-bag [ma...
Male, the He of a ...
Main, chief, princip...
Mane, the hair on the neck of a horse
Maize, Indian corn
Maze, a labyrinth
Mall, a wooden hammer
Maul, to beat grossly
Manner, custom
Manor, a jurisdiction
Mare, a female horse
Mayor, a magistrate
Marshal, a general offi-
Martial, warlike [cer
Marten, a large weasel, a kind of swallow
Martin, a man's name
Mead, a sweet liquor
Mede, a native of Me-
Meed, reward [dia
Mean, low, pitiful, sordid
Mien, deportment
Meat, flesh
Meet, fit
Mete, to measure
Medal, a coin
Meddle, to interfere
Meddler, an officious person
Medlar, a fruit
Melt, to make liquid
Milt, the roe of a fish
Message, an errand
Messuage, a house
Metal, gold, silver, &c.
Mettle, vigour, spirit
Meteor, a fiery body
Meter, one who mea-
Metre, poetry [sures

Mewl, to cry as a child
Mule, an animal
Mews, as a cat
Muse, to ponder
Might, power [cheese
Mite, an insect in
Mighty, powerful
Mity, full of mites
Mile, 8 furlongs
Moil, to toil or drudge
Miner, a worker in mines
Minor, one under age
Missal, a mass-book
Missile, that can be thrown
Moan, to lament
Mown, cut down
Moat, a ditch
Mote, an atom
Moor, a fen or marsh
More, greater
Mower, one who mows
Morning, before noon
Mourning, lamenting
Mus-lin, fine cotton cloth [mouth
Muzzling, tying the
Naval, relating to ships
Navel, part of the body
Naught, bad, worthless
Nought, nothing
Nay, not
Neigh, to cry as a horse
Near, nigh
Ne'er, never
Neither, not either
Nether, lower
None, not any
Nun, a religious maid
Oar, a thing to row
O'er, over [with
Ore, unrefined metal
Of, concerning
Off, distant from
Oh! an interjection of sorrow
Owe, to be indebted
One, the first in num-
Won, gained [ber
Order, rank, method
Ordure, animal dung
Pail, a wooden vessel
Pale, wan or white
Pain, torment
Pane, a square of glass
Pair, a couple
Pare, to cut or chip off
Payer, one who pays
Pear, a fruit
Palace, a royal house
Pallas, a heathen goddess [taste
Palate, the organ of
Palette, a painter's board
Pall, a funeral cloth
Paul, a man's name
Panel, a square of wainscot [saddle
Pannel, a kind of
Parasite, a flatterer
Parricide, a parent-killer
Parcel, a small bundle
Partial, biassed [man
Person, a man or wo-
Parson, a priest
Pastor, a minister
Pasture, grazing land
Patience, endurance
Patients, sick people
Patron, a benefactor
Pattern, a specimen
Pause, a stop
Paws, the feet of beasts
Peace, quietness
Piece, a part
Peak, the top of a thing
Pique, a grudge, ill-will
Peal, a ring of bells
Peel, to strip off the
Peer, a nobleman [skin
Pier, the column of an arch [ing
Pencil, a tool for draw-
Pensile, suspended
Penitence, repentance
Penitents, those who repent
Pilate, a man's name
Pilot, a guide at sea
Pint, half a quart
Point, a sharp end
Pistol, a small gun
Pistole, a Spanish coin
Plaice, a flat sea-fish
Place, locality, residence
Plaid, a highland garb
Play'd, acted [cere
Plain, even, blunt, sin-
Plane, a carpenter's
Plait, a fold [tool
Plate, wrought silver
Pleas, excuses
Please, to delight
Plum, a fruit [weight
Plumb, a leaden
Poach, to boil, to steal game [portico
Porch, an entrance, a
Poesy, poetry
Posy, a motto on a ring, a nosegay
Pole, a perch, the extremity of the earth
Poll, the head [mean
Poor, lean, indigent,
Pore, to look intensely
Poplar, a tall tree
Popular, loved by the people
Populace, the common people [ited
Populous, fully inhab-
Portion, a share
Potion, a draught
Poster, a courier
Posture, a position
Pour, to fall heavily
Power, might, authority [custom
Practice, use, habit,
Practise, to exercise
Praise, commendation
Prays, entreats
Preys, plunders
Pray, to beseech
Prey, booty
Precedent, an example
President, a governor
Precentor, a leader in a choir [stows
Presenter, one who be-
Presence, being present
Presents, gifts
Preyer, a robber
Prior, former, antecedent, first
Pries, scarches

Prize, a reward to merit
Principal, chief, capital
Principle, a first cause
Profit, gain
Prophet, an inspired person [woman
Quean, a worthless
Queen, a king's wife
Rabbet, a joint in carpentry
Rabbit, a furry animal
Radish, a garden root
Reddish, inclined to red [clouds
Rain, water from the
Reign, to rule as a king
Raise, to lift up
Rays, beams of light
Raze, to destroy
Raisin, a dried grape
Reason, a cause
Rap, to strike smartly
Wrap, to fold up
Rapine, plunder
Rapping, knocking
Wrapping, folding up
Razor, a tool to shave with [mark
Razure, a scratch, a
Read, to peruse [pipe
Reed, a plant, a small
Read, perused
Red, a colour
Reck, to regard
Wreck, destruction, loss
Reek, smoke, steam
Wreak, revenge, fury
Regimen, diet [soldiers
Regiment, a body of
Rest, ease
Wrest, to force
Retch, to vomit
Wretch, a worthless person [the glands
Rheum, moisture from
Room, a chamber
Rhone, the name of a
Roan, a colour [river
Rhyme, metre
Rime, hoar frost
Rice, Indian corn
Rise, advancement
Rigger, a fitter out
Rigour, severity
Right, just, true
Rite, a ceremony
Wright, a workman
Write, to express by letter
Ring, to strike a bell
Wring, to twist, to distress [lers
Road, a way for travel-
Rode, did ride
Row'd, did row
Roe, a female deer
Row, a line of things
Rote, words extempore
Wrote, did write [red
Wrought, manufactu-
Rough, uneven, stormy
Ruff, a linen ornament
Rues, repents
Ruse, artifice, cunning
Rung, sounded
Wrung, twisted
Rye, grain
Wry, distorted
Sail, a sheet made of canvass
Sale, an auction
Satire, keen language
Satyr, a sylvan god
Saver, one who saves
Saviour, the Redeemer
Savour, taste [wound
Scar, the mark of a
Scare, to frighten
Scene, a part of a play
Sean, a large fishing-
Seen, beheld [net
Scent, a smell
Sent, ordered away
Sea, the ocean
See, to behold
Seam, a joining
Seem, to appear
Seas, extensive waters
Sees, doth see
Seize, to lay hold of
Season, proper time
Seizing, taking possession [gion
Sects, parties in reli-
Sex, male and female
Seignior, the grand
Senior, elder [Turk
Sew, to work with a
So, thus [needle
Sow, to scatter seed
Sewer, a drain
Suer, one who entreats
Sure, certain
Shear, to clip
Sheer, clear, pure, real
Shire, a county
Shoar, a prop
Shore, the sea-coast
Sigher, one who sighs
Sire, a father
Sighs, deep sobs
Size, bulk, a glutinous substance
Sign, a token
Sine, a geometrical line
Sleight, dexterity
Slight, neglect
Sloe, a wild plum
Slow, dull, not speedy
Sole, a fish, part of a shoe [spirit
Soul, an immortal
Soar, to rise high
Sore, an ulcer
Sower, one who sows
Some, a part
Sum, the whole
Son, a male child [day
Sun, the luminary of
Spital, a charitable foundation
Spittle, saliva
Soon, speedy, quick
Swoon, to faint
Sord, a grassy turf
Sword, a sharp weapon
Stair, a step
Stare, an earnest look
Steal, to pilfer
Steel, hardened iron
Stile, steps into a field
Style, manner of writing
Subtle, artful
Suttle, the net weight
Subtler, more subtly
Suttler, one who sells provisions
Succour, help
Sucker, a young shoot
Suitor, a petitioner

Suture, a seam
Surplice, a white robe
Surplus, over and above
Tacks, small nails
Tax, tribute duty
Tail, the end of a thing
Tale. a story
Taint, an infection
Teint, a colour
Talents, faculties
Talons, claws
Tare, an allowance in weight, a plant
Tear, to rend [horses
Team, a set of cart
Teem, to abound [eye
Tear, water from the
Tier, a row of guns in
Tenor, purport [a ship
Tenure, condition of holding
Tierce, a kind of cask
Terse, smooth, neat, exact [them
Their, belonging to
There, in that place
Threw, flung, tossed
Through, by means of
Throne, a chair of state
Thrown, hurled
Thyme, an herb [sure
Time, duration, lei-
Tide, the flux and reflux of the sea
Tied, bound
To, unto
Toe, a part of the foot

Tow, hemp or flax dress-
Too, also [ed
Two, a couple
Told, related
Toll'd, rang [ment
Tongs, a fire instru-
Tongues, languages
Tour, a journey
Tower, a lofty building
Tray, a utensil [dice
Trey, the 3 at cards or
Treaties, conventions
Treatise, a discourse
Vale, a valley, a dale
Veil, a covering for the
Vain, fruitless [face
Vane, a weathercock
Vein, a blood-vessel
Valley, the space between two hills
Value, price, worth
Vial, a small bottle
Viol, a musical instrument [ter
Wade, to walk in wa-
Weigh'd, balanced, considered
Wail, to lament
Wale, a rising part
Whale, the largest of
Wain, a wagon [all fish
Wane, a decrease or decline [body
Waist, a part of the
Waste, a wanton destruction
Wait, to tarry
Weight, heaviness

Ware, goods
Wear, to have on
Were, plural of *was*
Where, at what place
Way, a road
Weigh, to balance
Whey, a beverage from
Weak, faint [milk
Week, seven days
Weal, prosperity
Wheal, a pustule
Wheel, a round body
Weather, state of the air [ram
Wether, a castrated
Whether, which of the two [crescence
Wen, a fleshy ex-
When, at what time
Whither, to what place
Wither, to decay
Which, this or that
Witch, a sorceress
While, mean time
Wile, a trick [grapes
Wine, the juice of
Whine, to moan
Whist, a game at cards
Wist, knew
White, a colour
Wight, an island
Wood, timber
Would, was willing
Wreath, to fold
Writhe, to distort
Yarn, spun wool
Yearn, to grieve
Yest, barm

TABLE XXII.

WORDS SPELT ALIKE, BUT PRONOUNCED DIFFERENTLY.

ábject	to abjéct	cómpact	to compáct	cóntrast	to contrást
ábsent	to absént	cómpound	to compóund	cónvent	to convént
ábstract	to abstráct	cómpress	to compréss	cónverse	to convérse
áccent	to accént	cóncert	to concért	cónvert	to convért
áffix	to affix	cóncrete	to concréte	cónvict	to convict
ássign	to assign	cónduct	to condúct	cónvoy	to convóy
áttribute	to attribute	cónfine	to confine	désert	to desért
áugment	to augmént	cónflict	to conflict	díscount	to discóunt
bómbard	to bombárd	cónserve	to conserve	déscant	to descánt
cément	to cemént	cónsort	to consórt	dígest	to digest
cólleague	to colléague	cóntest	to contest	éssay	to essáy
cóllect	to colléct	cóntract	to contráct	éxport	to expórt

MURRAY'S ENGLISH GRAMMAR.

ENGLISH GRAMMAR is the art of speaking and writing the English language with propriety.

It is divided into four parts, viz. ORTHOGRAPHY, ETYMOLOGY, SYNTAX, and PROSODY.

ORTHOGRAPHY.

LETTERS.

Orthography teaches the nature and power of letters, and the just method of spelling words.

A letter is the first principle, or least part of a word.

The letters of the English language, called the English Alphabet, are twenty-six in number.

These letters are the representatives of certain articulate sounds, the elements of the language. An articulate sound, is the sound of the human voice, formed by the organs of speech.

Letters are divided into vowels and consonants.

A vowel is an articulate sound, that can be perfectly uttered by itself; as, *a, e, o;* which are formed without the help of any other sound.

A consonant is an articulate sound, which cannot be perfectly uttered without the help of a vowel; as, *b, d, f, l;* which require vowels to express them fully.

The vowels are, *a, e, i, o, u,* and sometimes *w* and *y*.

W and *y* are consonants when they begin a word or syllable; but in every other situation they are vowels.

Consonants are divided into mutes and semi-vowels.

The mutes cannot be sounded *at all* without the aid of a vowel. They are *b, p, t, d, k,* and *c* and *g* hard.

The semi-vowels have an imperfect sound of themselves. They are *f, l, m, n, r, v, s, z, x,* and *c* and *g* soft.

Four of the semi-vowels, namely, *l, m, n, r,* are also distinguished by the name of *liquids*, from their readily uniting with other consonants, and flowing as it were into their sounds.

A diphthong is the union of two vowels, pronounced by a single impulse of the voice; as, *ea* in beat, *ou* in sound.

A triphthong, the union of three vowels, pronounced in like manner; as, *eau* in beau, *iew* in view.

A proper diphthong is that in which both the vowels are sounded; as, *oi* in voice, *ou* in ounce.

An improper diphthong has but one of the vowels sounded; as, *ea* in eagle, *oa* in boat.

SYLLABLES.

A syllable is a sound, either simple or compounded, pronounced by a single impulse of the voice, and constituting a word, or part of a word; as, a, an, ant.

Spelling is the art of rightly dividing words into their syllables; or of expressing a word by its proper letters.

WORDS.

Words are articulate sounds, used, by common consent, as signs of our ideas.

A word of one syllable is termed a monosyllable; a word of two syllables, a dissyllable; a word of three syllables, a trisyllable; and a word of four or more syllables, a polysyllable.

All words are either primitive or derivative.

A primitive word is that which cannot be reduced to any simpler word in the language; as, man, good, content.

A derivative word is that which may be reduced to another word in *English* of greater simplicity; as, manful, goodness, contentment, Yorkshire.

ETYMOLOGY.

The second part of Grammar is Etymology; which treats of the different sorts of words, their various modifications, and their derivation.

There are in English nine sorts of words, or, as they are commonly called, PARTS OF SPEECH; namely, the ARTICLE, the SUBSTANTIVE OR NOUN, the ADJECTIVE, the PRONOUN, the VERB, the ADVERB, the PREPOSITION, the CONJUNCTION, and the INTERJECTION.

1. An Article is a word prefixed to substantives to point them out,

and to show how far their signification extends; as, *a* garden, *an* eagle, *the* woman.

2. A Substantive or noun is the name of any thing that exists, or of which we have any notion; as, *London*, *man*, *virtue*.

A substantive may, in general, be distinguished by its taking an article before it, or by its making sense of itself; as, a *book*, the *sun*, an *apple*; *temperance*, *industry*, *chastity*.

3. An Adjective is a word added to a substantive, to express its quality; as, An *industrious* man, a *virtuous* woman.

An adjective may be known by its making sense with the addition of the word *thing*; as, a *good* thing, a *bad* thing; or of any particular substantive; as, a *sweet* apple, a *pleasant* prospect.

4. A Pronoun is a word used instead of a noun, to avoid the too frequent repetition of the same word; as, The man is happy; *he* is benevolent; *he* is useful.

5. A verb is a word which signifies to BE, to DO, or to SUFFER; as "I *am*, I *rule*, I *am ruled*."

A verb may generally be distinguished by its making sense with any of the personal pronouns, or, the word *to* before it; as, I *walk*, he *plays*, they *write*; or, to *walk*, to *play*, to *write*.

6. An Adverb is a part of speech joined to a verb, an adjective, and sometimes to another adverb, to express some quality or circumstance respecting it; as, he reads *well*; a *truly* good man; he writes *very correctly*.

An adverb may be generally known by its answering to the question, How? How much? When? or Where? as, in the phrase, "He reads *correctly*," the answer to the question, How does he read? is, *correctly*.

7. Prepositions serve to connect words with one another, and to show the relation between them; as, "He went *from* London *to* York," "she is *above* disguise;" "they are supported *by* industry."

A preposition may be known by its admitting after it a personal pronoun in the objective case; as, *with*, *for*, *to*, &c. will allow the objective case after them; with *him*, for *her*, to *them*, &c.

8. A Conjunction is a part of speech that is chiefly used to connect sentences; so as, out of two or more sentences, to make but one: it sometimes connects only words; as, "Thou *and* he are happy, *because* you are good." "Two *and* three are five."

9. An Interjection is a word used to express some passion or emotion of the mind; as, "Oh! I have alienated my friend; alas! I fear, for life."

ARTICLE.

An Article is a word prefixed to substantives, to point them out, and to show how far their signification extends; as, *a* garden, *an* eagle, *the* woman.

In English there are but two articles, *a* and *the*: *a* becomes *an* before a vowel, and before a silent *h*; as, *an* acorn, *an* hour. But if the *h* be sounded, the *a* only is to be used; as, *a* hand, *a* heart, *a* highway.

A or *an* is styled the indefinite article: it is used in a vague sense, to point out one single thing of the kind, in other respects indeterminate; as, "Give me *a* book;" "Bring me *an* apple."

The is called the definite article, because it ascertains what particular thing or things are meant; as, "Give me *the* book;" "Bring me *the* apples;" meaning some book, or apples, referred to.

A substantive without any article to limit it, is generally taken in its widest sense; as, "A candid temper is proper for man;" that is, for all mankind.

SUBSTANTIVE.

A Substantive or noun is the name of any thing that exists, or of which we have any notion; as, *London*, *man*, *virtue*.

Substantives are either proper or common.

Proper names or substantives, are the names appropriated to individuals; as *George*, *London*, *Thames*.

Common names, or substantives, stand for kinds containing many sorts, or for sorts containing many individuals under them; as, animal, man, tree, &c.

To substantives belong gender, number, and case; and they are all of the third person, when spoken *of*; and of the second, when spoken *to*: as, "Blessings attend us on every side: be grateful, children of men!" that is, "*ye* children of men."

Gender.

Gender is the distinction of nouns, with regard to sex. There are three genders, the Masculine, the Feminine, and the Neuter.

The masculine gender den

animals of the male kind; as, a man, a horse, a bull.

The feminine gender signifies animals of the female kind; as, a woman, a duck, a hen.

The neuter gender denotes objects which are neither males nor females; as, a field, a house.

Some substantives naturally neuter are, by a figure of speech, converted into the masculine or feminine gender; as, when we say of the sun, *he* is setting, and of a ship, *she* sails well, &c.

There are three methods of distinguishing the sex, viz.

1. By different words: as,

Male.	*Female.*
Bachelor.	Maid.
Boar.	Sow.
Boy.	Girl.
Brother.	Sister.
Buck.	Doe.
Bull.	Cow.
Bullock *or* Steer.	Heifer.
Cock.	Hen.
Dog.	Bitch.
Drake.	Duck.
Earl.	Countess.
Father.	Mother.
Friar.	Nun.
Gander.	Goose.
Hart.	Roe.
Horse.	Mare
Husband.	Wife.
King.	Queen.
Lad.	Lass.
Lord.	Lady.
Man.	Woman.
Master.	Mistress.
Milter.	Spawner.
Nephew.	Niece.
Ram.	Ewe.
Singer.	Songstress *or* Singer
Sloven.	Slut.
Son.	Daughter.
Stag.	Hind.
Uncle.	Aunt.
Wizard.	Witch.

2. By a difference of termination: as,

Male.	*Female.*
Abbot.	Abbess.
Actor.	Actress.
Administrator.	Administratrix.
Adulterer.	Adultress
Ambassador.	Ambassadress.
Arbiter.	Arbitress.
Baron.	Baroness.
Bridegroom.	Bride.
Benefactor.	Benefactress.
Caterer.	Cateress.
Chanter.	Chantress.
Conducter.	Conductress.
Count.	Countess.
Deacon.	Deaconess.
Duke.	Duchess.
Elector.	Electress.
Emperor.	Empress
Enchanter.	Enchantress.
Executor.	Executrix.
Governor.	Governess
Heir.	Heiress.
Hero.	Heroine.
Hunter.	Huntress.
Host.	Hostess.
Jew.	Jewess.
Landgrave	Landgravine.
Lion.	Lioness.
Marquis.	Marchioness.
Master.	Mistress.
Mayor.	Mayoress.
Patron.	Patroness.
Peer.	Peeress.
Poet.	Poetess.
Priest.	Priestess.
Prince.	Princess.
Prior.	Prioress.
Prophet.	Prophetess.
Protector.	Protectress.
Shepherd.	Shepherdess.
Songster.	Songstress.
Sorcerer.	Sorceress.
Sultan.	Sultaness, Sultana.
Tiger.	Tigress.
Traitor.	Traitress.
Tutor.	Tutoress.
Viscount.	Viscountess.
Votary.	Votaress.
Widower.	Widow.

3. By a noun, pronoun, or adjective, being *prefixed* to the substantive: as,

Male.	*Female.*
A cock-sparrow.	A hen-sparrow.
A man servant.	A maid-servant.
A he goat.	A she-goat.
A he-bear.	A she-bear
A male child.	A female child.
Male descendants.	Female descendants.

Nouns that are either masculine or feminine, or including both, may be properly called the common gender; as, *parent, child scholar, friend*.

Number.

Number is the consideration of an object, as one or more.

Substantives are of two numbers, the singular and the plural.

The singular number expresses but one object; as, a chair, a table.

The plural number signifies more objects than one; as, chairs, tables.

Some nouns, from the nature of the things which they express, are used only in the singular, others only in the plural form; as, wheat, pitch, gold, sloth, pride, &c., and bellows, scissors, ashes, riches, &c.

Some words are the same in both numbers; as, deer, sheep, swine, &c.

The plural number of nouns is generally formed by adding *s* to the singular; as, dove, doves; face, faces; thought, thoughts. But when the substantive singular ends in *x ch, sh*, or *ss*, or *s*, we add *es* in the plural; as, box, boxes; church, churches; lash, lashes; kiss, kisses• rebus, rebuses.

Nouns ending in *f* or *fe*, are generally rendered plural by the change of those terminations into *ves*; as, loaf, loaves; wife, wives. Those which end in *ff*, have the regular plural; as, ruff, ruffs.

Such as have *y* in the singular, with no other vowel in the same syllable, change it into *ies* in the plural; as, beauty, beauties; fly, flies: but the *y* is not changed, when there is another vowel in the syllable; as, key, keys; delay, delays.

Case.

In English, substantives have three cases, the Nominative, the Possessive, and the Objective.

The nominative case simply expresses the name of a thing, or the subject of the verb; as, "The *boy* plays;" "The *girls* learn."

The possessive case expresses the relation of property or possession; and has an apostrophe, with the letter *s* coming after it; as, "The scholar's duty;" "My father's house."

When the plural ends in *s*, the other *s* is omitted, but the apostrophe is retained; as, "On eagles' wings;" "The drapers' company."

Sometimes, also, when the singular terminates in *ss*, the apostrophic s is not added; as, "For goodness' sake;" "For righteousness' sake."

The objective case expresses the object of an action, or of a relation; and generally follows a verb active, or a preposition; as, "John assists Charles!" "They live in London."

English substantives are declined in the following manner:

	Singular.	*Plural.*
Nom. Case.	A Mother.	Mothers.
Poss Case.	A Mother's.	Mothers'.
Obj. Case.	A Mother.	Mothers.
Nom. Case.	The man.	The men.
Poss. Case.	The man's.	The men's.
Obj. Case	The man.	The men.

ADJECTIVES.

An adjective is a word added to a substantive, to express its quality; as, "An industrious man;" "A virtuous woman;" "A benevolent mind."

In English the adjective is not varied on account of gender, number, or case. Thus we say, "A careless boy;" "Careless girls."

The only variation which it admits, is that of the degrees of comparison.

There are commonly reckoned three degrees of comparison; the positive, comparative, and superlative.

The positive state expresses the quality of an object, without any increase or diminution; as, good, wise, great.

The comparative degree increases or lessens the positive in signification; as, wiser, greater, less wise.

The superlative degree increases or lessens the positive to the highest or lowest degree; as, wisest, greatest, least wise.

The simple word, or positive, becomes the comparative, by adding *r* or *er*; and the superlative, by adding *st* or *est*, to the end of it; as, wise, wiser, wisest; great, greater, greatest. And the adverbs *more* and *most*, placed before the adjective, have the same effect; as, wise, *more* wise, *most* wise.

Monosyllables, for the most part, are compared by *er* or *est*; and dissyllables by *more* and *most*; as, mild, milder, mildest; frugal, more frugal, most frugal.

Some words of very common use are irregularly formed; as, good, better, best; bad, worse, worst; little, less, least; much, or many, more, most; and a few others.

PRONOUNS.

A Pronoun is a word used instead of a noun, to avoid the too frequent repetition of the same word; as, "The man is happy;" "*he* is benevolent;" "*he* is useful."

There are three kinds of pronouns; viz., the Personal, the Relative, and the Adjective Pronouns.

Personal Pronouns.

There are five personal pronouns; viz., *I*, *thou*, *he*, *she*, *it*; with their plurals, *we*, *ye* or *you*, *they*.

Personal pronouns admit of person, number, gender, and case.

The persons of pronouns are three in each of the numbers, viz.

I, is the first person *Thou*, is the second person *He*, *she*, or *it*, is the third person	Sing.
We, is the first person *Ye*, or *you*, is the second person *They*, is the third person	Plural.

The numbers of pronouns, like those of substantives, are two; the singular and the plural; as, *I*, *thou*, *he*; *we*, *ye*, *they*.

Gender has respect only to the third person singular of the pronouns, *he*, *she*, *it*. *He* is masculine; *she* is feminine; *it* is neuter.

Pronouns have three cases; the nominative, the possessive, and the objective.

The objective case of a pronoun has, in general, a form different from that of the nominative or the possessive case.

The personal pronouns are thus declined:

First Person.

	Singular.	*Plural.*
Nominative.	I.	We.
Possessive.	Mine.	Ours.
Objective.	Me.	Us.

Second Person.

	Singular.	*Plural.*
Nominative.	Thou.	Ye *or* you.
Possessive.	Thine.	Yours.
Objective.	Thee.	You.

Third Person Masculine.

	Singular.	*Plural.*
Nominative.	He.	They.
Possessive.	His.	Theirs.
Objective.	Him.	Them

Third Person Feminine.

	Singular.	*Plural.*
Nominative.	She.	They.
Possessive.	Hers.	Theirs.
Objective.	Her.	Them.

Third Person Neuter.

	Singular.	*Plural.*
Nominative.	It.	They.
Possessive.	Its.	Theirs.
Objective.	It.	Them.

Relative Pronouns.

Relative Pronouns are such as relate, in general, to some word or phrase going before, which is thence called the antecedent: they are, *who*, *which*, and *that*; as, "The man is happy *who* lives *virtuously*."

What is a kind of compound relative, including both the antecedent and the relative, and is mostly equivalent to *that which*; as, "This is *what* I wanted;" that is to say, "*the thing which* I wanted."

Who is applied to persons, *which* to animals irrational and things inanimate; as, "He is a friend *who* is faithful in adversity;" "The *bird*, *which* sung so sweetly, is flown;" "This is the *tree*, *which* produces no fruit."

That, as a relative, is often used to prevent the too frequent repetition of *who* and *which*. It is applied to both persons and things; as, "He *that* acts wisely deserves praise;" "Modesty is a *quality that* highly adorns a woman."

Who is of both numbers, and is thus declined:

Singular and Plural.

Nominative.	Who.
Possessive.	Whose.
Objective.	Whom.

Who, *which*, *what*, are called *Interrogatives*, when they are used in asking questions; as, "*Who* is he?" "*Which* is the book?" "*What* are you doing?"

Adjective Pronouns.

Adjective pronouns are of a mixed nature, participating the properties both of pronouns and adjectives.

The adjective pronouns may be subdivided into four sorts, namely, the *possessive*, the *distributive*, the *demonstrative*, and the *indefinite*.

1. The *possessive* are those which relate to possession or property.

There are seven of them; viz. *my*, *thy*, *his*, *her*, *our*, *your*, *their*.

Mine and *thine*, instead of *my* and *thy*, were formerly used before a substantive or adjective, beginning with a vowel or a silent *h*; as, "Blot out all *mine* iniquities."

2. The *distributive* are those which denote the persons or things that make up a number, as taken separately and singly. They are *each*, *every*, *either*; as, "*Each* of his brothers is in a favourable situation;" "*Every* man must account for himself;" "I have not seen *either* of them."

3. The *demonstrative* are those which precisely point out the subjects to which they relate: *this* and *that*, *these* and *those*, are of this class; as, "*This* is true charity; *that* is only its image."

This refers to the nearest person or thing, and *that* to the more distant; as, "*This* man is more intelligent than *that*." *This* indicates the latter, or last mentioned; *that*, the former, or first mentioned; as, "Wealth and poverty are both temptations; *that* tends to excite pride, *this*, discontent."

4. The *indefinite* are those which express their subjects in an indefinite or general manner. The following are of this kind: *some*, *other*, *any*, *one*, *all*, *such*, *&c.*

Other is declined in the following manner:

	Singular.	*Plural.*
Nominative.	other	others.
Possessive.	other's	others'.
Objective.	other	others.

Verbs.

A verb is a word which signifies to *be*, to *do*, or to *suffer;* as, "I am, I rule, I am ruled."

Verbs are of three kinds; *active*, *passive*, and *neuter*. They are also divided into *regular*, *irregular*, and *defective*.

A *verb active* expresses an action, and necessarily implies an agent, and an object acted upon; as, to love, "I love Penelope."

A *verb passive* expresses a passion or suffering, or the receiving of an action; and necessarily implies an object acted upon, and an agent by which it is acted upon; as, to be loved; "Penelope is loved by me."

A *verb neuter* expresses neither action nor passion; but being, or a state of being; as, "I am, I sleep, I sit."

Auxiliary, or *helping verbs*, are those by the help of which the English verbs are principally conjugated; they are *do*, *be*, *have*, *shall*, *will*, *may*, *can*, with their variations; and *let*, and *must*, which have no variation.

To verbs belong *number*, *person*, and *tense*.

Number and Person.

Verbs have two numbers, the singular and the plural; as, "I love, we love."

In each number there are three persons; as,

	Singular.	*Plural.*
First Person.	I love.	We love.
Second Person.	Thou lovest.	Ye love.
Third Person.	He loves.	They love.

Moods.

Mood is a particular state or form of the verb, showing the manner in which the being, action, or passion is represented.

There are five moods of verbs, the *indicative*, the *imperative*, the *potential*, the *subjunctive*, and the *infinitive*.

The Indicative Mood simply indicates or declares a thing; as, "He loves; he is loved;" or it asks a question; as, "Does he love? Is he loved?"

The Imperative Mood is used for commanding, exhorting, entreating, or permitting; as, "Depart thou; mind ye; let us stay; go in peace."

The Potential Mood implies possibility, or liberty, power, will, or obligation; as, "It *may* rain; he *may* go or stay; I *can* ride; he *would* walk; they *should* learn."

The Subjunctive Mood represents a thing as contingent or uncertain, as under a condition, motive, wish, supposition, &c.; and is preceded by a conjunction, expressed or understood, and attended by another verb; as, "I will respect him, *though* he chide me;" "Were he good, he would be happy;" that is, "*if* he were good."

The Infinitive Mood expresses a thing in a general and unlimited manner, without any distinction of number or person; as, "to act, to speak, to be feared."

The Participle is a certain form of the verb, and derives its name from its participating, not only the properties of a verb, but also those of an adjective; as, "I am desirous of *knowing* him;" *Admired* and *applauded*, he became vain;" "*Having finished* his work, he submitted it," &c.

There are three Participles, the Present or Active, the Perfect or Passive, and the Compound Perfect; as, "loving, loved, having loved."

Tenses.

Tense, being the distinction of time, might seem to admit only of the present, past, and future; but to mark it more accurately, it is made to consist of six variations; viz. the *present*, the *imperfect*, the *perfect*, the *pluperfect*, and the *first* and *second future tenses*.

The Present Tense represents an action or event, as passing at the time in which it is mentioned; as, "I rule; I am ruled; I think; I fear."

The Imperfect Tense represents the action or event, either as past and finished, or as remaining unfinished at a certain time past; as, "I loved her for her modesty and virtue;" "They were travelling post when he met them."

The Perfect Tense not only refers to what is past, but also conveys an allusion to the present time; as, "I have finished my letter;" "I have seen the person that was recommended to me."

The Pluperfect Tense represents a thing not only as past, but also as prior to some other point of time specified in the sentence; as, "I had finished my letter before he arrived."

The First Future Tense represents the action as yet to come, either with or without respect to the precise time when; as, "The sun will rise to-morrow;" "I shall see them again."

The Second Future intimates that the action will be fully accomplished, at or before the time of another future action or event; as, "The two houses will have finished their business when the king comes to prorogue them."

The Conjugation of a verb is the regular combination of an arrangement of its several numbers, persons, moods, and tenses.

The conjugation of an active verb is styled the *active voice;* and that of a passive verb, the *passive voice.*

The auxiliary and active verb *To have,* is conjugated in the following manner:

TO HAVE.

Indicative Mood.

Present Tense.

Singular.	Plural.
1. *Pers.* I have.	1. We have.
2. *Pers.* Thou hast.	2. Ye *or* you have.
3. *Pers.* He, she, or it, hath *or* has.	3. They have.

Imperfect Tense.

Singular.	Plural.
1. I had.	1. We had.
2. Thou hadst.	2. Ye *or* you had.
3. He, &c. had.	3. They had.

Perfect Tense.

Singular.	Plural.
1. I have had.	1. We have had.
2. Thou hast had.	2. Ye *or* you have had.
3. He has had.	3. They have had.

Pluperfect Tense.

Singular.	Plural.
1. I had had.	1. We had had.
2. Thou hadst had.	2. Ye *or* you had had.
3. He had had.	3. They had had.

First Future Tense.

Singular.	Plural.
1. I shall *or* will have.	1. We shall *or* will have.
2. Thou shalt *or* wilt have.	2. Ye *or* you shall *or* will have.
3. He shall *or* will have.	3. They shall *or* will have.

Second Future Tense.

Singular.	Plural.
1. I shall have had.	1. We shall have had.
2. Thou wilt have had.	2. Ye *or* you will have had.
3. He will have had.	3. They will have had.

Imperative Mood.

Singular.	Plural.
1. Let me have.	1. Let us have.
2. Have thou, *or* do thou have.	2. Have ye, *or* do ye *or* you have.
3. Let him have.	3. Let them have.

Potential Mood.

Present Tense.

Singular.	Plural.
1. I may *or* can have.	1. We may *or* can have.
2. Thou mayst *or* canst have.	2. Ye *or* you may *or* can have.
3. He may *or* can have.	3. They may *or* can have.

Imperfect Tense.

Singular.	Plural.
1. I might, could, would, *or* should have.	1. We might, could, would, *or* should have.
2. Thou mightst, couldst, wouldst, *or* shouldst have.	2. Ye *or* you might could, would, *or* should have.
3. He might, could, would, *or* should have.	3. They might, could, would, *or* should have.

Perfect Tense.

Singular.	Plural.
1. I may *or* can have had.	1. We may *or* can have had.
2. Thou mayst *or* canst have had.	2. Ye *or* you may *or* can have had.
3. He may *or* can have had.	3. They may *or* can have had.

Pluperfect Tense.

Singular.	Plural.
1. I might, could, would, *or* should have had.	1. We might, could, would, *or* should have had.
2. Thou mightst, couldst, wouldst, *or* shouldst have had.	2. Ye *or* you might, could, would, *or* should have had.
3. He might, could, would, *or* should have had.	3. They might, could, would, *or* should have had.

Subjunctive Mood.

Present Tense.

Singular.	Plural.
1. If I have.	1. If we have.
2. If thou have.	2. If ye *or* you have.
3. If he have.	3. If they have.

Infinitive Mood.

Present. To have. *Perfect.* To have had.

Participles.

Present or Active.	Having.
Perfect or Passive.	Had.
Compound Perfect.	Having had.

The auxiliary and neuter verb *To be*, is conjugated as follows:

TO BE.

Indicative Mood.

Present Tense.

Singular.	Plural.
1. I am.	1. We are.
2. Thou art.	2. Ye *or* you are.
3. He, she, *or* it is.	3. They are.

Imperfect Tense.

Singular.	Plural.
1. I was.	1. We were.
2. Thou wast.	2. Ye *or* you were.
3. He was.	3. They were.

Perfect Tense.

Singular.	Plural.
1. I have been.	1. We have been.
2. Thou hast been.	2. Ye *or* you have been.
3. He hath *or* has been.	3. They have been.

Pluperfect Tense.

Singular.	Plural.
1. I had been.	1. We had been.
2. Thou hadst been.	2. Ye *or* you had been.
3. He had been.	3. They had been.

First Future Tense.

Singular.	Plural.
1. I shall *or* will be.	1. We shall *or* will be.
2. Thou shalt *or* wilt be.	2. Ye *or* you shall *or* will be.
3. He shall *or* will be.	3. They shall *or* will be.

Second Future Tense.

Singular.	Plural.
1. I shall have been.	1. We shall have been.
2. Thou wilt have been.	2. Ye *or* you will have been.
3. He will have been.	3. They will have been.

Imperative Mood.

Singular.	Plural.
1. Let me be.	1. Let us be.
2. Be thou, *or* do thou be.	2. Be ye *or* you, *or* do ye be.
3. Let him be.	3. Let them be.

Potential Mood.

Present Tense.

Singular.	Plural.
1. I may *or* can be.	1. We may *or* can be.
2. Thou mayst *or* canst be.	2. Ye *or* you may *or* can be.
3. He may *or* can be.	3. They may *or* can be.

Imperfect Tense.

Singular.	Plural.
1. I might, could, would, *or* should be.	1. We might, could, would, *or* should be.
2. Thou mightst, couldst, wouldst, *or* shouldst be.	2. Ye *or* you might, could, would, *or* should be.
3. He might, could, would, *or* should be.	3. They might, could, would, *or* should be.

Perfect Tense.

Singular.	Plural.
1. I may *or* can have been.	1. We may *or* can have been.
2. Thou mayst *or* canst have been.	2. Ye *or* you may *or* can have been.
3. He may *or* can have been.	3. They may *or* can have been.

Pluperfect Tense.

Singular.	Plural.
1. I might, could, would, *or* should have been.	1. We might, could, would, *or* should have been.
2. Thou mightst, couldst, wouldst, *or* shouldst have been.	2. Ye *or* you might, could, would, *or* should have been.
3. He might, could, would, *or* should have been.	3. They might, could, would, *or* should have been.

Subjunctive Mood.

Present Tense.

Singular.	Plural
1. If I be.	1. If we be.
2. If thou be.	2. If ye *or* you be.
3. If he be.	3. If they be.

Imperfect Tense.

Singular.	Plural.
1. If I were.	1. If we were.
2. If thou wert.	2. If ye or you were.
3. If he were.	3. If they were.

Infinitive Mood.

Present Tense.	To be.
Perfect.	To have been.

Participles.

Present.	Being.
Perfect.	Been.
Compound Perfect.	Having been.

Of the Conjugation of Regular Verbs.

Active.

Verbs Active are called Regular when they form their imperfect tense of the indicative mood, and their perfect participle, by adding to the verb *ed*, or *d* only, when the verb ends in *e*; as,

Present.	Imperfect.	Perf. Participle.
I favour.	I favoured.	Favoured.
I love.	I loved.	Loved.

A Regular Active Verb is conjugated in the following manner:

TO LOVE.

Indicative Mood.

Present Tense.

Singular.	Plural.
1. I love.	1. We love.
2. Thou lovest.	2. Ye *or* you love.
3. He, she, *or* it loveth *or* loves.	3. They love.

Imperfect Tense.

Singular.	Plural.
1. I loved.	1. We loved.
2. Thou lovedst.	2. Ye *or* you loved.
3. He loved.	3. They loved.

Perfect Tense.

Singular.	Plural.
1. I have loved.	1. We have loved.
2. Thou hast loved.	2. Ye *or* you have loved.
3. He hath *or* has loved.	3. They have loved.

Pluperfect Tense.

Singular.	Plural.
1. I had loved.	1. We had loved.
2. Thou hadst loved.	2. Ye *or* you had loved.
3. He had loved.	3. They had loved.

First Future Tense.

Singular.	Plural.
1. I shall *or* will love.	1. We shall *or* will love.
2. Thou shalt *or* wilt love.	2. Ye *or* you shall *or* will love.
3. He shall *or* will love.	3. They shall *or* will love.

Second Future Tense.

Singular.	Plural.
1. I shall have loved.	1. We shall have loved.
2. Thou wilt have loved.	2. Ye *or* you will have loved.
3. He will have loved.	3. They will have loved.

Imperative Mood.

Singular.	Plural.
1. Let me love.	1. Let us love.
2. Love thou, *or* do thou love.	2. Love ye *or* you, *or* do ye love.
3. Let him love.	3. Let them love.

Potential Mood.

Present Tense.

Singular	Plural.
1. I may *or* can love.	1. We may *or* can love.
2. Thou mayst *or* canst love.	2. Ye *or* you may *or* can love.
3. He may *or* can love.	3. They may *or* can love.

Imperfect Tense.

Singular.	Plural.
1. I might, could, would, *or* should love.	1. We might, could, would, *or* should love.
2. Thou mightst, couldst, wouldst, *or* shouldst love.	2. Ye *or* you might could, would, *or* should love.
3. He might, could, would, *or* should love.	3. They might, could, would, *or* should love.

Perfect Tense.

Singular.	Plural.
1. I may *or* can have loved.	1. We may *or* can have loved.
2. Thou mayst *or* canst have loved.	2. Ye *or* you may *or* can have loved.
3. He may *or* can have loved.	3. They may *or* can have loved.

Pluperfect Tense.

Singular.	Plural.
1. I might, could, would, *or* should have loved.	1. We might, could, would, *or* should have loved.
2. Thou mightst, couldst, wouldst, *or* shouldst have loved.	2. Ye *or* you might, could, would, *or* should have loved.
3. He might, could, would, *or* should have loved.	3. They might, could, would, *or* should have loved.

Subjunctive Mood.

Present Tense.

Singular.	Plural.
1. If I love.	1. If we love.
2. If thou love.	2. If ye *or* you love.
3. If he love.	3. If they love.

Infinitive Mood.

Present. To love. *Perfect.* To have loved.

Participles.

Present.	Loving.
Perfect.	Loved.
Compound Perfect.	Having loved.

Passive

Verbs Passive are called Regular when they form their perfect participle by the addition of *d* or *ed* to the verb; as, from the verb, "To love," is formed the passive "I am loved, I was loved, I shall be loved," &c.

A passive verb is conjugated by adding the perfect participle to the auxiliary *to be*, through all its changes of number, person, mood, and tense, in the following manner:

TO BE LOVED.

Indicative Mood.

Present Tense.

Singular.	Plural.
1. I am loved.	1. We are loved.
2. Thou art loved.	2. Ye *or* you are loved.
3. He is loved.	3. They are loved.

Imperfect Tense.

Singular.	Plural.
1. I was loved.	1. We were loved.
2. Thou wast loved	2. Ye *or* you were loved.
3. He was loved.	3. They were loved.

Perfect Tense.

Singular.	Plural.
1. I have been loved.	1. We have been loved.
2. Thou hast been loved.	2. Ye *or* you have been loved.
3. He hath *or* has been loved.	3. They have been loved.

Pluperfect Tense.

Singular.	Plural.
1. I had been loved.	1. We had been loved.
2. Thou hadst been loved.	2. Ye *or* you had been loved.
3. He had been loved.	3. They had been loved.

First Future Tense.

Singular.	Plural.
1. I shall *or* will be loved.	1. We shall *or* will be loved.
2. Thou shalt *or* wilt be loved.	2. Ye *or* you shall *or* will be loved.
3. He shall *or* will be loved.	3. They shall *or* will be loved.

Second Future Tense.

Singular.	Plural.
1. I shall have been loved.	1. We shall have been loved.
2. Thou wilt have been loved.	2. Ye *or* you will have been loved.
3. He will have been loved.	3. They will have been loved.

Imperative Mood.

Singular.	Plural.
1. Let me be loved.	1. Let us be loved.
2. Be thou loved, *or* do thou be loved.	2. Be ye *or* you loved, *or* do ye be loved.
3. Let him be loved.	3. Let them be loved.

Potential Mood.

Present Tense.

Singular.	Plural.
1. I may *or* can be loved.	1. We may *or* can be loved.
2. Thou mayst *or* canst be loved.	2. Ye *or* you may *or* can be loved.
3. He may *or* can be loved.	3. They may *or* can be loved.

Imperfect Tense.

Singular.	Plural.
1. I might, could, would, *or* should be loved.	1. We might, could, would, *or* should be loved.
2. Thou mightst, couldst, wouldst, *or* shouldst be loved.	2. Ye *or* you might, could, would, *or* should be loved.
3. He might, could, would, *or* should be loved.	3. They might, could, would, *or* should be loved.

Perfect Tense.

Singular.	Plural.
1. I may *or* can have been loved.	1. We may *or* can have been loved.
2. Thou mayst *or* canst have been loved.	2. Ye *or* you may *or* can have been loved.
3. He may *or* can have been loved.	3. They may *or* can have been loved.

Pluperfect Tense.

Singular.	Plural.
1. I might, could, would, *or* should have been loved.	1. We might, could, would, *or* should have been loved.
2. Thou mightst, couldst, wouldst, *or* shouldst have been loved.	2. Ye *or* you might, could, would, *or* should have been loved.
3. He might, could, would, *or* should have been loved.	3. They might, could, would, *or* should have been loved.

Subjunctive Mood.

Present Tense.

Singular.	Plural.
1. If I be loved.	1. If we be loved.
2. If thou be loved.	2. If ye *or* you be loved.
3. If he be loved.	3. If they be loved.

Imperfect Tense.

Singular.	Plural.
1. If I were loved.	1. If we were loved.
2. If thou wert loved.	2. If ye *or* you were loved.
3. If he were loved.	3. If they were loved.

Infinitive Mood.

Present Tense.	To be loved.
Perfect.	To have been loved

Participles.

Present.	Being loved.
Perfect or *Passive.*	Loved.
Compound Perfect.	Having been loved.

IRREGULAR VERBS.

Irregular Verbs are those which do not form their imperfect tense, and their perfect participle, by the addition of *d* or *ed* to the verb; as,

Present.	Imperfect.	Perf. or Pass. Part.
I begin,	I began,	begun.
I know,	I knew,	known.

Irregular Verbs are of various sorts.

1. Such as have the present and imperfect tenses, and perfect participle the same; as,

Present.	Imperfect.	Perfect Part.
Cost,	cost,	cost.
Put,	put,	put.

2. Such as have the imperfect tense, and perfect participle, the same; as,

Present.	Imperfect.	Perfect Part.
Abide,	abode,	abode.
Sell,	sold,	sold.

3. Such as have the imperfect tense, and perfect participle, different; as,

Present.	Imperfect.	Perfect Part.
Arise,	arose,	arisen.
Blow,	blew,	blown

The following list of the irregular verbs will, it is presumed, be found both comprehensive and accurate.

Present.	Imperfect.	Perf. or Pass. Part.
Abide,	abode,	abode.
Am,	was,	been.
Arise,	arose,	arisen.
Awake,	awoke, R.	awaked.
Bear, *to bring forth,*	bare,	born.
Bear, *to carry,*	bore,	borne.
Beat,	beat,	beaten, beat.
Begin,	began,	begun.
Bend,	bent,	bent.
Bereave,	bereft, R.	bereft, R.
Beseech,	besought,	besought.
Bid,	bid, bade,	bidden, bid.
Bind,	bound,	bound.
Bite,	bit,	bitten, bit.
Bleed,	bled,	bled.
Blow,	blew,	blown.
Break,	broke,	broken.
Breed,	bred,	bred.
Bring,	brought,	brought.
Build,	built,	built.
Burst,	burst,	burst.
Buy,	bought,	bought.
Cast,	cast,	cast.
Catch,	caught, R.	caught, R.
Chide,	chid,	chidden, chid.
Choose,	chose,	chosen.
Cleave, *to stick or adhere.*	REGULAR.	
Cleave, *to split,*	clove *or* cleft,	cleft, cloven.
Cling,	clung,	clung.
Clothe,	clothed,	clad, R.
Come,	came,	come.
Cost,	cost,	cost.
Crow,	crew, R.	crowed.
Creep,	crept,	crept.
Cut,	cut,	cut.
Dare, *to venture,*	durst,	dared.
Dare, R. *to challenge.*		
Deal,	dealt, R.	dealt, R.
Dig,	dug, R.	dug, R.
Do,	did,	done.
Draw,	drew,	drawn.
Drive,	drove,	driven.
Drink,	drank,	drunk.
Dwell,	dwelt, R.	dwelt, R.
Eat,	eat, *or* ate,	eaten.
Fall,	fell,	fallen.
Feed,	fed,	fed.
Feel,	felt,	felt.
Fight,	fought,	fought.
Find,	found,	found.
Flee,	fled,	fled.
Fling,	flung,	flung.
Fly,	flew,	flown.
Forget,	forgot,	forgotten, forgot.
Forsake,	forsook,	forsaken.
Freeze,	froze,	frozen.
Get,	got,	got.
Gild,	gilt, R.	gilt, R.
Gird,	girt, R.	girt, R.
Give,	gave,	given.
Go,	went,	gone.
Grave,	graved,	graven.
Grind,	ground,	ground.
Grow,	grew,	grown.
Have,	had,	had.

Present.	Imperfect.	Perf. or Pass. Part.
Hang,	hung, R.	hung, R.
Hear,	heard,	heard.
Hew,	hewed,	hewn, R.
Hide,	hid,	hidden, hid
Hit,	hit,	hit.
Hold,	held,	held.
Hurt,	hurt,	hurt.
Keep,	kept,	kept.
Knit,	knit, R.	knit, R.
Know,	knew,	known.
Ladê,	laded,	laden.
Lay,	laid,	laid.
Lead,	led,	led.
Leave,	left,	left.
Lend,	lent,	lent.
Let,	let,	let.
Lie, *to lie down,*	lay,	lain.
Load,	loaded,	laden, R.
Lose,	lost,	lost.
Make,	made,	made.
Meet,	met,	met.
Mow,	mowed,	mown, R.
Pay,	paid,	paid.
Put,	put,	put.
Read,	read,	read.
Rend,	rent,	rent.
Rid,	rid,	rid.
Ride,	rode,	rode, *or* ridden.
Ring,	rung, rang,	rung.
Rise,	rose,	risen.
Rive,	rived,	riven.
Run,	ran,	run.
Saw,	sawed,	sawn, R.
Say,	said,	said.
See,	saw,	seen.
Seek,	sought,	sought.
Sell,	sold,	sold.
Send,	sent,	sent.
Set,	set,	set.
Shake,	shook,	shaken.
Shape,	shaped,	shaped, shapen
Shave,	shaved,	shaven, R.
Shear,	sheared,	shorn.
Shed,	shed,	shed.
Shine,	shone, R.	shone, R
Show,	showed,	shown.
Shoe,	shod,	shod.
Shoot,	shot,	shot.
Shrink,	shrunk,	shrunk.
Shred,	shred,	shred.
Shut,	shut,	shut.
Sing,	sung, sang,	sung.
Sink,	sunk, sank,	sunk.
Sit,	sat,	sat.
Slay,	slew,	slain.
Sleep,	slept,	slept.
Slide,	slid,	slidden.
Sling,	slung,	slung.
Slink,	slunk,	slunk.
Slit,	slit, R.	slit, *or* slitted
Smite,	smote,	smitten.
Sow,	sowed,	sown, R.
Speak,	spoke,	spoken.
Speed,	sped,	sped.
Spend,	spent,	spent.
Spill,	spilt, R.	spilt, R.
Spin,	spun,	spun.
Spit,	spit, spat,	spit, spitten.
Split,	split,	split.
Spread,	spread,	spread.
Spring,	sprung, sprang,	sprung.
Stand,	stood,	stood.
Steal,	stole,	stolen.

Present.	Imperfect.	Perf. or Pass. Part.
Stick,	stuck,	stuck.
Sting,	stung,	stung.
Stink,	stunk,	stunk.
Stride,	strode, *or* strid,	stridden.
Strike,	struck,	struck, *or* stricken.
String,	strung,	strung.
Strive,	strove,	striven.
Strow, *or* Strew,	strowed, *or* strewed,	strown, strowed, strewed.
Swear,	swore,	sworn.
Sweat,	swet, R.	swet, R.
Swell,	swelled,	swollen, R.
Swim,	swum, swam,	swum.
Swing,	swung,	swung.
Take,	took,	taken.
Teach,	taught,	taught.
Tear,	tore,	torn.
Tell,	told,	told.
Think,	thought,	thought.
Thrive,	throve, R.	thriven.
Throw,	threw,	thrown.
Thrust,	thrust,	thrust.
Tread,	trod,	trodden.
Wax,	waxed,	waxen, R.
Wear,	wore,	worn.
Weave,	wove,	woven.
Weep,	wept,	wept.
Win,	won,	won.
Wind,	wound,	wound.
Work,	wrought,	wrought, *or* worked.
Wring,	wrung,	wrung.
Write,	wrote,	written.

The verbs which are conjugated regularly, as well as irregularly, are marked with an R. Those preterits and participles which are first mentioned in the list, seem to be the most eligible.

Defective Verbs.

Defective Verbs are those which are used only in some of their moods and tenses; as, *am, was, been; can, could; may, might; shall, should; will, would, &c.*

Adverbs.

An Adverb is a part of speech joined to a verb, an adjective, and sometimes to another adverb, to express some quality or circumstance respecting it; as, "He reads *well;*" "A *truly* good man;" "He writes *very* correctly."

Some adverbs are compared thus: "Soon, sooner, soonest; often, oftener, oftenest." Those ending in *ly*, are compared by *more* and *most;* as, "Wisely, more wisely, most wisely."

The following are a few of the Adverbs:

Once	lately	perhaps
now	presently	indeed
here	often	not
lastly	much	how
before	quickly	more

Prepositions.

Prepositions serve to connect words with one another, and to show the relation between them. They are, for the most part, set before nouns and pronouns: as, "He went *from* London *to* York;" "She is *above* disguise;" "They are supported *by* industry."

The following is a list of the principal prepositions:

Of	under	up
to	through	down
for	above	before
by	below	behind
with	between	off
in	beneath	on *or* upon
into	from	among
within	beyond	after
without	at	about
over	near	against

Conjunction.

A Conjunction is a part of speech that is chiefly used to connect sentences; so as out of two or more sentences, to make but one. It sometimes connects only words.

Conjunctions are principally divided into two sorts; the *copulative* and *disjunctive.*

The conjunction copulative serves to connect or to continue a sentence, by expressing an addition, a supposition, a cause, &c.; as, "He *and* his brother reside in London;" "I will go, *if* he will accompany me;" "You are happy, *because* you are good."

The Conjunction Disjunctive serves, not only to connect and continue the sentence, but also to express opposition of meaning in different degrees: as, "*Though* he was frequently reproved, *yet* he did not reform;" "They came with her, *but* went away without her."

The following is a list of the principal conjunctions:

The *Copulative.* And, that, both, for, therefore, if, then, since, because, wherefore.

The *Disjunctive.* But, than, though, either, or, as, unless, neither, nor, lest, yet, notwithstanding.

Interjections.

An Interjection is a word used to express some passion or emotion of the mind: as, "Oh! I have alienated my friend; Alas! I fear, for life."

The following are some of the Interjections: O! pish! heigh! lo! behold! ah! tush! fie! hush! hail!

Of Derivation.

Words are derived from one another in various ways, viz.

1. Substantives are derived from verbs: as, from "to love" comes "lover."

2. Verbs are derived from substantives, adjectives, and sometimes from adverbs: as, from "salt" comes "to salt;" from "warm" comes "to warm;" from "forward" comes "to forward."

3. Adjectives are derived from substantives; as, from "health" comes "healthy."

4. Substantives are derived from adjectives; as, from "white" comes "whiteness."

5. Adverbs are derived from adjectives; as, from "base" comes "basely."

SYNTAX.

The third part of Grammar is *Syntax*, which treats of the agreement and construction of words in a sentence.

A sentence is an assemblage of words, forming a complete sense.

Sentences are of two kinds, *simple* and *compound.*

A simple sentence has in it but one subject, and one finite verb; as, "Life is short."

A compound sentence consists of two or more simple sentences connected together: as, "Life is short, and art is long;" "Idleness produces want, vice, and misery."

A phrase is two or more words rightly put together, making sometimes part of a sentence, and sometimes a whole sentence.

The principal parts of a simple sentence are, the subject, the attribute, and the object.

The subject is the thing chiefly spoken of; the attribute is the thing or action affirmed or denied of it; and the object is the thing affected by such action.

The nominative denotes the subject, and usually goes before the verb or attribute; and the word or phrase, denoting the object, follows the verb; as, "A wise man governs his passions." Here a *wise man* is the subject; *governs*, the attribute, or thing affirmed; and *his passions*, the object.

Syntax principally consists of two parts, Concord and Government.

Concord is the agreement which one word has with another, in gender, number, case, or person.

Government is that power which one part of speech has over another, in directing its mood, tense, or case.

RULE I.

A verb must agree with its nominative case, in number and person: as, "I learn;" "Thou art improved;" "The birds sing."

RULE II.

Two or more nouns, &c. in the singular number, joined together by a copulative conjunction, expressed or understood, have verbs, nouns, and pronouns, agreeing with them in the plural number: as, "Socrates and Plato *were* wise: *they* were the most eminent philosophers of Greece;" "The sun that rolls over our heads, the food that we receive, the rest that we enjoy, daily *admonish* us of a superior and superintending power.

RULE III.

The conjunction disjunctive has an effect contrary to that of the conjunction copulative; for, as the verb, noun, or pronoun, is referred to the preceding terms taken separately, it must be in the singular number: as, "Ignorance or negligence *has* caused this mistake;" "John, or James, or Joseph, *intends* to accompany me;" "There *is*, in many minds, neither knowledge nor understanding."

RULE IV.

A noun of multitude, or signifying many, may have a verb or pronoun agreeing with it, either of the singular or plural number; yet not without regard to the import of the word, as conveying unity or plurality of idea: as, "The meeting *was* large;" "The parliament *is* dissolved;" "The nation *is* powerful;" "My people *do* not consider: *they* have not known me;" "The multitude eagerly *pursue* pleasure as *their* chief good;" "The council *were* divided in *their* sentiments."

RULE V.

Pronouns must always agree with their antecedents, and the nouns for which they stand in gender and number: as, "This is the friend *whom* I love;" "That is the vice *which* I hate;" "The king and the queen *had* put on their robes;" "The moon appears, and *she* shines, but the light is not *her* own."

The relative is of the same person as the antecedent, and the verb agrees with it accordingly: as, "Thou *who lovest* wisdom;" "I, *who speak* from experience."

RULE VI.

The relative is the nominative case to the verb, when no nominative comes between it and the verb: as, "The master *who* taught us;" "The trees *which* are planted."

When a nominative comes between the relative and the verb, the relative is governed by some word in its own member of the sentence: as, "He *who* preserves me, to *whom* I owe my being, *whose* I am, and *whom* I serve, is eternal."

RULE VII.

When the relative is preceded by two nominatives of different persons, the relative and verb may agree in person with either, according to the sense: as, "I am the man *who command* you;" or, "I am the man *who commands* you."

RULE VIII.

Every adjective, and every adjective pronoun, belongs to a substantive, expressed, or understood: as, "He is a *good*, as well as a *wise man;*" "*Few are happy;*" that is, "*persons;*" "*This* is a pleasant walk;" that is, "*This walk is,*" &c.

Adjective pronouns must agree, in number, with their substantives: as, "This book, these books; that sort, those sorts; another road, other roads."

RULE IX.

The article *a* or *an* agrees with nouns in the singular number only, individually or collectively: as, "A Christian, an infidel, a score, a thousand."

The definite article *the* may agree with nouns in the singular or plural number: as, "the garden, the houses, the stars."

The articles are often justly omitted: when used they should be properly applied, according to their distinct nature; as, "Gold is corrupting; The sea is green; A lion is bold."

RULE X.

One substantive governs another signifying a different thing, in the possessive or genitive case: as, "My father's house;" "Man's happiness;" "Virtue's reward."

RULE XI.

Active verbs govern the objective case: as, "Truth ennobles *her;*" "She comforts *me;*" "They support *us;*" "Virtue rewards *her followers.*"

RULE XII.

One verb governs another that follows it, or depends upon it, in the infinitive mood: as, "Cease *to do* evil; learn *to do* well;" "We should be prepared *to render* an account of our actions."

The preposition *to*, though generally used before the latter verb, is sometimes properly omitted: as, "I heard him say it;" instead of, "*to* say it."

RULE XIII.

In the use of words and phrases which, in point of time, relate to each other, a due regard to that relation should be observed. Instead of saying, "The Lord *hath given*, and the Lord hath taken away;" we should say, "The Lord *gave*, and the Lord *hath taken* away." Instead of, "I *know* the family more than twenty years;" it should be, "I *have known* the family more than twenty years."

RULE XIV.

Participles have the same government as the verbs from which they are derived: as, "I am weary with *hearing him;*" "She is *instructing us;*" "The tutor is *admonishing Charles.*"

RULE XV.

Adverbs, though they have no government of case, tense, &c. require an appropriate situation in the sentence, viz., for the most part before adjectives, after verbs active or neuter, and frequently between the auxiliary and the verb as, "He made a *very sensible* discourse; he *spoke unaffectedly* and *forcibly;* and *was attentively heard* by the whole assembly."

RULE XVI.

Two negatives, in English, destroy one another, or are equivalent to an affirmative: as, "*Nor* did they *not* perceive him;" that is, "they did perceive him;" "His language, though inelegant, is *not ungrammatical;*" that is, "it is grammatical."

RULE XVII.

Prepositions govern the objective case: as, "I have heard a good character *of her;*" "*From him* that is needy turn not away;" "A word to the wise is sufficient *for them;*" "We may be good and happy *without riches.*"

RULE XVIII.

Conjunctions connect the same moods and tenses of verbs, and cases of nouns and pronouns: as, "Candour is *to be approved and practised;*" "If thou sincerely *desire and* earnestly *pursue* virtue, she *will* assuredly *be found* by thee, *and prove* a rich reward;" "The master taught *her and me* to write;" "*He and she* were school-fellows."

RULE XIX.

Some conjunctions require the indicative, some the subjunctive mood, after them. It is a general rule, that, when something contingent or doubtful is implied, the subjunctive ought to be used: as, "*If* I *were* to write, he would not regard it;" "He will not be pardoned, *unless* he *repent.*"

Conjunctions that are of a positive and absolute nature, require the indicative mood. "*As* virtue *advances, so* vice *recedes.*" "He is healthy *because* he *is* temperate."

RULE XX.

When the qualities of different things are compared, the latter noun or pronoun is not governed by the conjunction *than* or *as*, but agrees with the verb, or is governed by the verb or the preposition, expressed or understood: as, "Thou art wiser than I;" that is, "than I am." "They loved him more than me;" i. e. "more than they loved me;" "The sentiment is well expressed by Plato, but much better by Solomon than him;" that is, "than by him."

RULE XXI.

To avoid disagreeable repetitions, and to express our ideas in few words, an ellipsis, or omission of some words, is frequently admitted. Instead of saying, "He was a learned man, he was a wise man, and he was a good man;" we use the ellipsis, and say, "He was a learned, wise, and good man."

When the omission of words would obscure the sentence, weaken its force, or be attended with an impropriety, they must be expressed. In the sentence, "We are apt to love who love us," the word *them* should be supplied. "A beautiful field and trees," is not proper language. It should be, "Beautiful fields and trees;" or, "A beautiful field and fine trees."

RULE XXII.

All the parts of a sentence should correspond to each other: a regular and dependent construction, throughout, should be carefully preserved. The following sentence is therefore inaccurate: "He was more beloved, but not so much admired as Cinthio." It should be, "He was more beloved than Cinthio, but not so much admired."

PROSODY.

Prosody consists of two parts: the former teaches the true pronunciation of words, comprising *accent, quantity, emphasis, pause,* and *tone;* and the latter, the laws of *versification.*

Accent.

Accent is the laying of a peculiar stress of the voice on a certain letter or syllable in a word, that it may be better heard than the rest, or distinguished from them: as, in the word *presúme,* the stress of the voice must be on the letter *u,* and second syllable *súme,* which takes the accent.

Quantity.

The quantity of a syllable is that time which is occupied in pronouncing it. It is considered as long or short.

A vowel or syllable is long when the accent is on the vowel, which occasions it to be slowly joined, in pronunciation, to the following letter: as, "Fāll, bāle, mōōd, hōūse, fēature."

A syllable is short when the accent is on the consonant, which occasions the vowel to be quickly joined to the succeeding letter; as, "an′t, bon′net, hun′ger."

A long syllable requires double the time of a short one, in pronouncing it: thus, "Māte" and "Nōte" should be pronounced as slowly again as, "Măt" and "Nŏt."

Emphasis.

By emphasis is meant a stronger and fuller sound of voice, by which we distinguish some word or words on which we design to lay particular stress, and to show how it affects the rest of the sentence. Sometimes the emphatic words must be distinguished by a particular tone of voice, as well as by a greater stress.

Pauses.

Pauses or rests, in speaking and reading, are a total cessation of the voice, during a perceptible, and, in many cases, a measurable space of time.

Tones.

Tones are different both from emphasis and pauses; consisting in the modulation of the voice, the notes or variations of sound which we employ, in the expression of our sentiments.

Versification.

Versification is the arrangement of a certain number and variety of syllables, according to certain laws.

Rhyme is the correspondence of the last sound of one verse, to the last sound or syllable of another.

PUNCTUATION

Is the art of dividing a written composition into sentences, or parts of sentences, by points or stops, for the purpose of marking the different pauses which the sense and an accurate pronunciation require.

The Comma represents the shortest pause; the Semicolon a pause double that of the comma; the Colon, double that of the semicolon; and the Period, double that of the colon.

The points are marked in the following manner:

The Comma ,	The Colon :
The Semicolon ;	The Period .

Comma.

The Comma usually separates those parts of a sentence, which, though very closely connected in sense, require a pause between them; as, "I remember, with gratitude, his love and services." "Charles is beloved, esteemed, and respected."

Semicolon.

The Semicolon is used for dividing a compound sentence into two or more parts, not so closely connected as those which are separated by a comma, nor yet so little dependent on each other as those which are distinguished by a colon; as, "Straws swim on the surface; but pearls lie at the bottom."

Colon.

The Colon is used to divide a sentence into two or more parts, less connected than those which are separated by a semicolon; but not so independent as separate, distinct sentences; as, "Do not flatter yourselves with the hope of perfect happiness: there is no such thing in the world."

Period.

When a sentence is complete and independent, and not connected in construction with the following sentence, it is marked with a period; as, "Fear God. Honour the king. Have charity towards all men."

Besides the points which mark the pauses in discourse, there are others that denote a different modulation of voice, in correspondence to the sense. These are,

The Interrogative point, ?
The Exclamation point, !
The Parenthesis, ( )

as, "Are you sincere?" "How excellent is a grateful heart!"

"Know then this truth, (enough for man
to know),
Virtue alone is happiness below."

The following characters are also frequently used in composition:

An Apostrophe, marked thus ' ; as, "tho', judg'd."

A Caret, marked thus ^ ; as,
am
"I diligent."
^

A Hyphen, which is thus marked - ; as, "Lap-dog, to-morrow."

The Acute Accent, marked thus ´; as, "Fáncy." The Grave Accent, thus `; as, "Fàvour."

The proper mark to distinguish a long syllable is this ¯; as, "Rōsy:" and a short one this ˘; as, "Fŏlly." This last mark is called a Breve.

A Diæresis, thus marked ¨, shows that two vowels form separate syllables, as, "Creätor."

A Section is thus marked §.

A Paragraph, thus ¶.

A Quotation has two inverted commas at the beginning, and two direct ones at the end of a phrase or passage; as,

"The proper study of mankind is man."

Crotchets or Brackets serve to inclose a particular word or sentence. They are marked thus [].

An Index or Hand ☞ points out a remarkable passage.

A Brace } unites three poetical lines; or connects a number of words, in prose, with one common term.

An Asterisk or little star * directs the reader to some note in the margin.

An Ellipsis is thus marked —— ; as, "K——g," for King.

An Obelisk, which is marked thus †, and Parallels thus ‖, together with the letters of the alphabet, and figures, are used as references to the margin.

CAPITALS.

The following words should begin with capitals:

1. The first word of every book, chapter, letter, paragraph, &c.

2. The first word after a period, and frequently after the notes of interrogation and exclamation.

3. The names of the Deity; as, God, Jehovah, the Supreme Being, &c.

4. Proper names of persons, places, ships, &c.

5. Adjectives derived from the proper names of places; as, Grecian, Roman, English, &c.

6. The first word of an example, and of a quotation in a direct form; as, "Always remember this ancient maxim, 'Know thyself.'"

7. The first word of every line in poetry.

8. The pronoun *I*, and the interjection *O!*

9. Words of particular importance; as, the Reformation, the Restoration, the Revolution.

ROMAN FIGURES.

1	I.	13	XIII.	45	XLV.	200	CC.
2	II.	14	XIV.	50	L.	300	CCC.
3	III.	15	XV.	55	LV.	400	CCCC.
4	IV.	16	XVI.	60	LX.	500	D.
5	V.	17	XVII.	65	LXV.	600	DC.
6	VI.	18	XVIII.	70	LXX.	700	DCC.
7	VII.	19	XIX.	75	LXXV.	800	DCCC.
8	VIII.	20	XX.	80	LXXX.	900	DCCCC.
9	IX.	25	XXV.	85	LXXXV.	1000	M.
10	X.	30	XXX.	90	XC.		
11	XI.	35	XXXV.	95	XCV.	1842.	
12	XII.	40	XL.	100	C.	MDCCCXLII.	

NUMERATION.

Units	1
Tens	1 2
Hundreds	1 2 3
Thousands	1 , 2 3 4
Tens of Thousands	1 2 , 3 4 5
Hundreds of Thousands	1 2 3 , 4 5 6
Millions	1 , 2 3 4 , 5 6 7
Tens of Millions	1 2 , 3 4 5 , 6 7 8
Hundreds of Millions	1 2 3 , 4 5 6 , 7 8 9

The seventh figure, as above, constitutes millions, six more would be billions, six more trillions, and so on for every six figures, to quadrillions, quintillions, sextillions, septillions, octillions, nonillions, &c.

MULTIPLICATION TABLE.

Twice 1 are 2	3 times 1 are 3	4 times 1 are 4	5 times 1 are 5	6 times 1 are 6	7 times 1 are 7	8 times 1 are 8	9 times 1 are 9	10 times 1 are 10	11 times 1 are 11	12 times 1 are 12
2.. 4	2.. 6	2.. 8	2..10	2..12	2.. 14	2.. 16	2.. 18	2.. 20	2.. 22	2.. 24
3.. 6	3.. 9	3..12	3..15	3..18	3.. 21	3.. 24	3.. 27	3.. 30	3.. 33	3.. 36
4.. 8	4..12	4..16	4..20	4..24	4.. 28	4.. 32	4.. 36	4.. 40	4.. 44	4.. 48
5..10	5..15	5..20	5..25	5..30	5.. 35	5.. 40	5.. 45	5.. 50	5.. 55	5.. 60
6 12	6..18	6..24	6..30	6..36	6.. 42	6.. 48	6.. 54	6.. 60	6.. 66	6.. 72
7..14	7..21	7..28	7..35	7..42	7.. 49	7.. 56	7.. 63	7.. 70	7.. 77	7.. 84
8..16	8..24	8..32	8..40	8..48	8.. 56	8.. 64	8.. 72	8.. 80	8.. 88	8.. 96
9..18	9..27	9. 36	9..45	9..54	9.. 63	9.. 72	9.. 81	9.. 90	9.. 99	9..108
10..20	10..30	10..40	10..50	10..60	10.. 70	10.. 80	10.. 90	10..100	10..110	10..120
11..22	11..33	11..44	11..55	11..66	11.. 77	11.. 88	11.. 99	11..110	11..121	11..132
12..24	12..36	12..48	12..60	12..72	12.. 84	12.. 96	12..108	12..120	12..132	12..144
13..2[illegible]	13..39	13..52	13..65	13..78	13.. 91	13..104	13..117	13..130	13..143	13..156
14..28	14..42	14..56	14..70	14..84	14.. 98	14..112	14..126	14..140	14..154	14..168
15..30	15..45	15..60	15..75	15..90	15..105	15..120	15..135	15..150	15 .165	15..180
16..32	16..48	16..64	16..80	16..96	16..112	16..128	16..144	16..160	16..176	16..192
17..34	17..51	17..68	17..85	17..102	17..119	17..13	17..153	17..170	17..187	17..204
18..36	18..54	18..72	18..90	18..108	18..126	18..144	18..162	18..180	18..198	18..216
19..38	19..57	19..76	19..95	19..114	19..133	19..152	19 .171	19..190	19..209	19..228
20..40	20 .60	20..80	20 .100	20..120	20..140	20..160	20..180	20..200	20 220	20..240

MONEY.

Farthings.		d.
2	are	0½
3	....	0¾
4	....	1
5	....	1¼
6	....	1½
7	....	1¾
8	....	2
9	....	2¼
10	....	2½
11	....	2¾
12	....	3
13	....	3¼

Farthings.		d.
14	are	3½
15	....	3¾
16	....	4
17	....	4¼
18	....	4½
19	....	4¾
20	....	5
21	....	5¼
22	....	5½
23	....	5¾
24	....	6
28	....	7

Farthings.		£.	s.	d.
32	are	0	0	8
36	....	0	0	9
40	....	0	0	10
44	....	0	0	11
48	....	0	1	0
96	....	0	2	0
120	....	0	2	6
240	....	0	5	0
480	....	0	10	0
960	....	1	0	0
1920	....	2	0	0
2880	....	3	0	0

MONEY.—(*Continued.*)

Pence.		s.	d.	Pence.		£.	s.	d.	Shillings.		£.	s.	Shillings.		£.	s.
12	are	1	0	120	......	0	10	0	20	are	1	0	200	are	10	0
20	......	1	8	130	......	0	10	10	30	......	1	10	250	......	12	10
24	......	2	0	132	......	0	11	0	40	......	2	0	300	......	15	0
30	......	2	6	140	......	0	11	8	50	......	2	10	350	......	17	10
36	......	3	0	144	......	0	12	0	60	......	3	0	400	......	20	0
40	......	3	4	150	......	0	12	6	70	......	3	10	450	......	22	10
48	......	4	0	156	......	0	13	0	80	......	4	0	500	......	25	0
50	......	4	2	160	......	0	13	4	90	......	4	10	650	......	32	10
60	......	5	0	170	......	0	14	2	100	......	5	0	750	......	37	10
70	......	5	10	180	......	0	15	0	110	......	5	10	850	......	42	10
72	......	6	0	190	......	0	15	10	120	......	6	0	950	......	47	10
80	......	6	8	200	......	0	16	8	130	......	6	10	1000	......	50	0
84	......	7	0	240	......	1	0	0	140	......	7	0	1500	......	75	0
90	......	7	6	480	......	2	0	0	150	......	7	10	2000	......	100	0
96	......	8	0	1200	......	5	0	0	160	......	8	0	2500	......	125	0
100	......	8	4	2400	......	10	2	0	170	......	8	10	3000	......	150	0
108	......	9	0	4800	......	20	0	0	180	......	9	0	4000	......	200	0
110	......	9	2	5000	......	20	16	8	190	......	9	10	5000	......	250	0

VALUE OF FOREIGN COINS IN BRITISH MONEY.

FRENCH.	s.	d.	SPANISH.	s.	d.	GERMAN.	s.	d.
Sous	0	$0\frac{1}{2}$	Quartil		$\frac{43}{136}$	Cruitzer	0	$0\frac{7}{15}$
Livres	0	10	Rial	0	$5\frac{3}{8}$	Florin	2	4
Franc	0	$10\frac{1}{8}$	Pictarine......	0	$10\frac{3}{4}$	Rix-dollar ...	3	6
Ecu	5	0	Piastre.........	3	7			
ouis d'Or	16	8	Dollar	4	6			
Old ditto.........	20	0	Ducat	4	$11\frac{1}{2}$	PORTUGUESE.		
FLEMISH.			Pistole	16	9			
Grot	0	$\frac{21}{40}$	RUSSIAN.			Vintin	0	$0\frac{7}{20}$
Stiver	0	$1\frac{1}{20}$	Copec	0	$0\frac{27}{50}$	Crusade	2	3
Schelling	0	$6\frac{3}{10}$	Altin...........	0	$1\frac{31}{50}$	Milrea	5	7
Guilder	1	9	Ruble	4	6	Moidore......	27	0
Pound	10	6						

PRACTICE TABLES.

Aliquot Parts of a

s.	d.		*Pound.*	d.		*Shilling.*	cwt.	qr.		*Ton.*
10	0	is	1-half	6	... is ...	1-half	10	0	is	1-half
6	8	...	1-3rd	4	....	1-3rd	5	0	...	1-4th
5	0	...	1-4th	3	....	1-4th	4	0	...	1-5th
4	0	...	1-5th	2	....	1-6th	2	2	...	1-8th
3	4	...	1-6th	$1\frac{1}{2}$	....	1-8th	2	0	...	1-10th
2	6	...	1-8th	1	....	1-12th	1	1	...	1-16th
2	0	...	1-10th			*Penny.*	1	0	...	1-20th
1	8	...	1-12th	$\frac{1}{2}$	....	1-half				*Cwt.*
1	4	...	1-15th	$\frac{1}{4}$	....	1-fourth	qr.	lbs.		
1	3	...	1-16th	lbs.		*Quarter.*	2 or	56	...	1-half
1	0	...	1-20th	14	....	1-half	1 ...	28	...	1-4th
0	8	...	1-30th	7	....	1-4th	0 ...	16	...	1-7th
0	6	...	1-40th	4	....	1-7th	0 ...	14	...	1-8th
0	4	...	1-60th	$3\frac{1}{2}$	....	1-8th	0 ...	8	...	1-14th
0	3	...	1-80th	2	....	1-14th	0 ...	7	...	1-16th
0	2	...	1-120th	1	....	1-28th	0 ...	4	...	1-28th
0	1	...	1-240th							

TABLE OF WEIGHTS AND MEASURES

APOTHECARIES' WEIGHT.

20 Grains make	1 Scruple.
3 Scruples	1 Dram.
8 Drams	1 Ounce.
12 Ounces	1 Pound.

Apothecaries mix their medicines by this weight, but buy and sell their drugs by Avoirdupoise weight.

The Apothecaries' pound and ounce and the pound and ounce Troy, are the same, only differently divided and sub-divided.

STANDARD TROY WEIGHT.

4 Grains make	1 Carat.
6 Carats, or 24 Grains	1 Penny-weight.
20 Pennyweights	1 Ounce.
12 Ounces	1 Pound.
25 Pounds	1 Quarter.
100 Pounds	1 Hundred weight.
20 Hundred weight	1 Ton of gold or silver.

Gold, Silver, Jewels, Amber, Precious Stones, Electuaries, and all Liquids are weighed by this weight.—The proportion of a pound Troy, to a pound Avoirdupoise, is as 14 to 17. The former containing 5760 Grains, and the latter 7000.

The standard for gold coin is 22 carats of fine gold, and 2 carats of copper melted together; for silver is 11 oz. 2 dwts. of fine silver, and 18 dwts. of alloy, which is now coined in 66s. instead of 62s. as formerly.

AVOIRDUPOISE WEIGHT.

16 Drams make	1 Ounce.
16 Ounces	1 Pound.
28 Pounds	1 Quarter.
4 Qrs. or 112 lbs.	1 Hund. weight.
20 Hundred weight	1 Ton.

By this weight are weighed all goods that are of a coarse or drossy nature; as, Pitch, Tar, Rosin, Tin, Iron, &c.; all Grocery and Chandlery wares, Silks, Bread, and all Metals but Gold and Silver. Some Silks are weighed by the great pound of 24 ounces, others by the common pound of 16 ounces. One pound Avoirdupoise contains 14 ounces, 11 pennyweights, 16 grains Troy.

WOOL WEIGHT.

7 Pounds make	1 Clove.
2 Cloves, or 14 lbs.	1 Stone.
2 Stones, or 28 lbs.	1 Tod.
6½ Tods	1 Wey
2 Weys	1 Sack.
12 Sacks	1 Last.
12 Score, or 240 lbs.	1 Pack.

A stone of different goods, and at different places, varies from 8 lbs. to 20 lbs. In the Midland districts it means 14 lbs.

Wool is weighed by Wool weight only.

HAY AND STRAW.

36 Pounds make	1 Truss of Straw.
56 Pounds	1 Truss of old Hay.
60 Pounds	1 Truss of new Hay
36 Trusses	1 Load.

STANDARD MEASURES OF CAPACITY,

In all of which the Gallon is the same; which Gallon, as well for liquids as dry goods not measured by heaped measure, contains 10 lbs. Avoirdupoise of distilled water, weighed in the air at 62 degrees of Farenheit's Thermometer, the Barometer being at 30 inches; and is the only standard measure of capacity, from which all other measures of capacity are computed.

ALE AND BEER MEASURE.

2 Pints make	1 Quart.
4 Quarts	1 Gallon.
9 Gallons	1 Firkin of Ale or Beer.
2 Firkins	1 Kilderkin.
2 Kilderkins	1 Barrel.
1½ Barrel	1 Hogshead.
2 Barrels	1 Puncheon.
3 Barrels	1 Butt.

In London they formerly computed but 8 gallons to the firkin of ale, and 32 to the barrel; but now, in all parts of England, the firkin of either ale or beer contains 9 gallons, and the barrel 36 gallons.

The imperial gallon contains $277\frac{274}{1000}$ cubic inches, and is 1-5th larger than the old wine gallon, 1-60th smaller than the beer gallon, and 1-57th larger than that used for dry goods.

WINE MEASURE.

4 Gills make	1 Pint.
2 Pints	1 Quart.
4 Quarts	1 Gallon.
10 Gallons	1 Anchor of Brandy.
18 Gallons	1 Rundlet.
31½ Gallons	½ a Hogshead.
42 Gallons	1 Tierce.
63 Gallons	1 Hogshead.
84 Gallons	1 Puncheon.
2 Hogsheads or 126 Gallons	1 Pipe or Butt.
2 Pipes or 252 Gallons	1 Tun.

In some parts of the country, a gill is reckoned half a pint.

Pipes vary in quantity, according to the kinds of wine they contain; viz., a pipe of Lisbon, 117 gallons, ditto of Port, 115, ditto of Sherry, 108, ditto of Vidonia, 100, ditto of Madeira, 92, ditto of Bucellas, 96.

German wines are sold by the single or double Auhn, of 30 or 60 gallons.

French wines are usually sold in bottles.

DRY MEASURE.

2 Pints make	1 Quart.
2 Quarts	1 Pottle.
2 Pottles	1 Gallon.
2 Gallons	1 Peck.
4 Pecks	1 Bushel.
2 Bushels	1 Strike.
4 Bushels	1 Coomb.
2 Coombs	1 Quarter.
4 Quarters	1 Chaldron.
4 Quarters	1 Wey or Load.
2 Weys	1 Last.

By this measure are measured all kinds of grain; such as Barley, Wheat, Oats, Pease, &c. which are stricken with a stick having an even surface from end to end.—The standard bushel contains 2218 cubic inches and a fifth, and measures 19½ inches in diameter, and 8¼ inches deep.

CLOTH MEASURE.

2¼ Inches make	1 Nail.
4 Nails	1 Quarter.
3 Quarters	1 Flemish Ell.
4 Quarters	1 Yard.
5 Quarters	1 English Ell.
6 Quarters	1 French Ell.

Scotch and Irish Linens, Woollens, Wrought Silks, Muslin, Cloths, Ribands, Cords, Tapes, &c. are measured by the yard; Dutch Linens by the ell English, and tapestry by the Flemish ell.

LONG MEASURE.

3 Barley Corns make	1 Inch.
3 Inches	1 Hand.*
10 Inches	1 Span.
12 Inches	1 Foot.
3 Feet	1 Yard.
5 Feet	1 Pace.
6 Feet	1 Fathom.
5½ Yards	1 Rod, Pole, or Perch.
4 Rods	1 Chain of Land.
40 Poles	1 Furlong.
8 Furlgs. or 1760 yds.	1 Mile.
3 Miles	1 League.
60 Geographical, or 69½ English Statute Miles	1 Degree.

360 Degrees the Circumference of the Globe.

Distances, lengths, heights, depths, &c of places or things, are measured by this measure.

* Horses are measured by the hand of 4 Inches.

A Mile in different Countries varies considerably.

	Yards.
The English mile contains	1760
The Russian ditto	1100
The Irish and Scotch ditto	2200
The Italian ditto	1467
The Polish ditto	4400
The Spanish ditto	5028
The German ditto	5866
The Swedish and Danish ditto	7233
The Hungarian ditto	8800

In France they measure by the mean league of 3666 yards.

SOLID, OR CUBIC MEASURE.

1728 Inches make	1 solid Foot.
27 Feet	1 Yard or Load.
40 Feet of unhewn Timber, or 50 ft. of hewn do.	1 Ton or Load.
108 Feet	1 Stack of Wood.
128 Feet	1 Cord of Wood

A cube is a solid body, containing length, breadth, and thickness. A cubic number is produced by being multiplied twice into itself.

LAND OR SQUARE MEASURE.

144 Square Inches	1	Square Foot.
9 Square Feet ...	1	Square Yard.
100 Feet	1	Sq. Flooring.
272¼ Feet, or 30¼ Yards ...	1	Rod of Brick-work.
16 Poles	1	Chain.
40 Rods, Poles, or Perches	1	Rood.
4 Roods, or 10 Chains, or 160 Rods, or 4840 Yds. or 100,000 Links	1	Acre of Land.
640 Acres	1	Square Mile.
30 Acres	1	Yd. of Land.
100 Acres	1	Hide of Land.
40 Hides	1	Barony.

A square is a figure of four equal sides and angles. A square number is produced by being multiplied into itself.

Painting, plastering, flooring, plumbing, tiling, glazing, &c. are measured by this measure. — It also ascertains the superficial contents by the length and breadth.

In measuring land, a chain is made use of, called "Gunter's Chain," which consists of 100 links, and measures 4 poles, or 22 yards, or 66 feet.

PAPER.

20 Sheets make	1	Quire of Outsides.
24 Sheets	1	Quire of Insides.
25 Sheets	1	Quire Printer's.
20 Quires	1	Ream.
2 Reams	1	Bundle.
10 Reams	1	Bale.

In a Ream of Paper there are two outsides or damaged quires.

TIME.

60 Seconds make	1	Minute.
60 Minutes	1	Hour.
12 Hours	1	Working Day.
24 Hours	1	Natural Day.
7 Days	1	Week.
4 Weeks or 28 Days	1	Lunar Month.
52 Weeks 1 Day, or 13 Lunar Months 1 Da.	1	Year.
365 Days 6 Hours	1	Julian Year.
365 Days 5 Hours 48 Min. 57 Sec. 39 Thirds	1	Solar Year.

The Number of Days in Each Month.

January	31	July	31
February ...	28	August	31
March	31	September ...	30
April	30	October	31
May	31	November ...	30
June	30	December ...	31

To know the Days in each Month.

Thirty days hath September,
April, June, and November;
February hath twenty-eight alone;
All the rest have thirty-one,
Except in Leap-year, then's the time,
February's days are twenty-nine.

The Quarter-Days.

Lady-day	25th March.
Midsummer-day	24th June.
Michaelmas-day	29th September.
Christmas-day ...	25th December.

CUSTOMARY WEIGHTS AND MEASURES.

Almonds, seron, cwt. 1¼ to ...cwt.	2
———, basket, cwt. 1¼ to...	1½
———, (Jordan), box ...... lbs.	25
Annatto, case, nearly ....cwt.	2¼
Arsenic, cask, about	4
Ashes, American, cask, 3½ to	5
———, St. Petersburgh, cask	10
Ballast, pig...................... lbs.	56
Beef (Irish) tierce of 38 pieces or...................... lbs.	304
——, barrel, 25 pieces of 8 lbs.	200
——, firkin, 25 pieces of 4 lbs.	100
Beer or Ale, barrel ......imp. gals.	36
——, hogshead	54
Brandy, hogshead, 45 to	60
———, puncheon, 100 to	110
———, ¼ cask, 20 to......	25
Bricks, load .... No.	500
Bristles, cask .... cwt.	10
Bullion, bar, lbs. 15 to ...... lbs.	30
Burgundy pitch, stand ...... cwt.	1¼
Butter, firkin...................... lbs.	56
———, tub......................	84
———, barrel......................	224
Camphor, box, about .... cwt.	1
Canvass, bolt, ells 28, or ... yds.	35
Cassia, chest .... lbs.	60
Cider, pipe, 100 to......imp. gals.	118
Cinnamon, bale .... lbs.	92½
Clover seed, cask, cwt. 7 to...cwt.	9
—————, sack, cwt. 2 to ...	3½
Cloves, matt, about .... lbs.	80
———, chest	200

Coals, London chaldron ...cwt. 25½
——, Newcastle do. of 3 wains 52½
————, estimated for boats at 53
——, keel of 8 N. chaldrons tons 21
Cochineal, seron .... lbs. 140
Cocoa, bag, about .... cwt. 1
——, cask 1¼
Cod fish, quintal .... lbs. 112
Coffee, tierce, cwt. 5 to ....cwt. 7
——, barrel, cwt. 1 to 1½
——, bag, cwt. 1¼ to 1½
——, Mocha, bale, cwt. 2 to 2½
————, robin, cwt. 1 to 1½
Copperas, hhd., cwt. 16 to ... 20
Cotton Wool (Virginia, Carolina, Georgia, W. Indies), bale, lbs. 300 to ....lbs. 310
—— (New Orleans, Alabama), 400 to 500
—— (E. India), bale, 320 to 360
—— (Brazil), bale, 160 to 200
—— (Egyptian), bale, 180 to 280
Currants, butt, cwt. 15 to ...cwt. 20
——, caroteel, cwt. 5 to 9
Feathers, bale, about 1
Figs (Faro), frail, lbs. 32, (Malaga) ....lbs. 56
—— (Turkey), drum 24
Flax (Russia), bale or matt, cwt. 5 to ....cwt. 6
—— (do.) 12 head bobbins...lbs. 126
—— (Dutch), matt 126
—— (Flemish), bale 224
Flour, peck or stone 14
——, boll of 10 pecks or stones 140
——, sack of 2 bolls 280
——, barrel 196
Galls, sack ....cwt. 3½
Geneva, piece, about...imp. gals. 116
Ginger (Jamaica), barrel, about ....cwt. 1
—— (Barbadoes), bag 1¼
—— (East India), bag 1
Gum, Arabic (E. I.) chest ... 6
——, (Turkey), chest 4
Gunpowder, barrel ....lbs. 100
Hay or Straw, load........trusses 36
—— truss ....lbs. 56
————, new to Sept. 1 60
Straw, truss 36
Hemp, bale, nearly ....cwt. 20
Herrings, barrel ...... imp. gals. 26⅔
——, cran 37½
——, cade ....No. 500
Honey, gallon ....lbs. 12
Hops, pocket, cwt. 1½ to ......cwt. 2
——, bag, nearly 2½
Indigo (E. I.), chest, about 3½ maunds, or ....lbs. 260
—— (Guatamala), seron... 250

Lac dye, chest ....cwt. 4
Lead (London, Hull), fodder 19½
—— (Black), cask, about 11½
Liquorice, juice, case, nearly 1½
Mace, case, about 1¼
Madder, cask, cwt. 15 to 23
Magnesia, chest 1
Meal (see Flour).
Molasses, puncheon, cwt. 10 to 12
Mustard, casks ....lbs. 18 and 36
Nutmegs, cask ....lbs. 200
Nuts (Barcelona), bag 126
—— (Messina), bag, cwt. 1½ to cwt. 1¾
Oil, tun ....wine gals. 252
———— ....imp. gals. 210
Olive oil, chest of 60 flasks 125
————, jar 25
Opium, chest, (E. I.), 2 maunds, or ....lbs. 149⅓
——, Turkey 136
Paper, quire ....sheets 24
——, ream ....quires 20
Parchment, roll ....skins 60
Pepper (black), Company's bag, ...lbs. 316
——, free trade bags lbs. 28, 56 112
—— (white), bag, about...cwt. 1½
Pilchards, barrel ..... imp. gals. 41⅔
Pimento, bag, about ....cwt. 1
Plums, ¼ box, about ....lbs. 20
——, carton 9
Pork (Irish), tierce, 80 pieces, or 320
——, barrel, army, 52 do. or 208
————, mess, 50 do. or 200
——, firkin, ... 25 do. or 100
Prunes, barrel, cwt. 1 to ......cwt. 3
Quicksilver, bottle, about ...lbs. 84
Rags (Hamburgh), bag ......cwt. 2½
——, (Mediterranean), bale, cwt. 4½ to 5
Raisins, drum, about ....lbs. 24
——, cask, Malaga ....cwt. 1
————, Turkey 2½
——, box, Malaga ....lbs. 22
————, Valencia 26
Rice (East In.), bag, about cwt. 1½
—— American, cask 6
Rosin, barrel, about 2
Rum, puncheon, gals. 90 to gals. 100
——, hogshead, do. 45 to 50
Sago, chest ....cwt. 1¾
——, bag 1
Salmon, box, lbs. 120 to......lbs. 130
Saltpetre (East India) bag, cwt. 1½
———— (refined), barrel...lbs. 112
Shellac, chest, cwt. 1 to ......cwt. 3
Smalts, barrel 3
Soap, chest 3¼
—— (soft), barrel of 4 firkins, lbs. 256

Soda, cask, cwt. 3 to ....cwt. 4
Sugar (W.I.), hhd., cwt. 13 to 16
——— tierce, cwt. 7 to......... 9
——— (Mauritus), matt or bag, cwt. 1 to .... $1\frac{1}{2}$
——— (East I.), bag, cwt. 1 to $1\frac{3}{4}$
Sugar Candy, box, about......lbs. 70
Sumach, bag, cwt. $1\frac{1}{2}$ to ......cwt. 2
Tallow, cask, about............... 9
Tapioca, barrel, about .... $1\frac{1}{2}$
Tar, barrel,...............imp. gals. $26\frac{1}{4}$
Tea, chest, Congou, about ...lbs. 84
———, Hyson, lbs. 60 to 80
Tiles, load ....No. 1000
Tobacco, hogshead, cwt. 12 to cwt. 18
Tragacanth, case, about ...... $2\frac{1}{2}$
Turpentine, barrel, cwt. 2 to $2\frac{1}{2}$
Vermillion, bag ....lbs. 50
Walnuts, bag ....cwt. 1
Whiskey (Scottish), puncheon,......imperial gals. 112 to 120
——— hogshead,...gals. 55 to 60
Wine, *standard gauges.* imp. gals.
———, pipe of port............... 115
——— Lisbon 117
——— Cape 92
Wine, pipe of Madeira imp. gals. 92
——— Teneriffe ... 100
———, butt of Sherry ... 108
———, hogshead of Claret 46
———, aum of Hoc......... 30
Wood, load, rough timber, ... cubic ft. 40
———, hewn...... 50
———, cord of fire wood is 4 feet long, 4 feet broad, and 8 feet deep.
Wool, sack of 2 weys, or 13 tods ....lbs. 364
———, last, ...sacks 12
———, pack ....lbs. 240
———, German bale, about 350
Yarn *(cotton)* thread ......inches 54
———, skein, or rap of 80 threads ....yds. 120
———, hank of 7 skeins 840
———, spindle of 18 hanks... 15,120
Yarn *(linen)* thread ......inches 90
———, heer of 2 cuts or 240 threads, ...yds. 600
———, spindle of 24 heers ... 14,400
———, bundle of $4\frac{1}{6}$ spindles 60,000

ON THE ART OF NUMBERING.

Figures are, 1 2 3 4 5 6 7 8 9, to which we add the cipher 0; and by these ten characters all numbers may be fully expressed.

The reading, writing, valuing, or expressing numbers, we call Numeration.

The common affections of all numbers are, Addition, Subtraction, Multiplication, and Division; which are called the Rules in Arithmetic.

Addition teaches to add or cast up several numbers together in one whole or total sum.—Subtraction teaches to take one number from another, and to know the remainder.—Multiplication shows, at one operation, the product of several sums added together.—Division shows how to separate any number into as many parts as you please. These four rules are called the Fundamental Rules; because no questions in this science can be wrought without them.

Reduction teaches to reduce numbers from one denomination to another, in coin, in weight, or measure.

The Rule of Three is either, single, double, direct, or inverse.—The Single Rule has three terms given to find a fourth; and the Double Rule has five terms given to find a sixth.—The direct rule requires a direct operation; and the Inverse Rule an Inverted operation.

All the other rules in Arithmetic are more or less dependent on the Rule of Three.

Fractions are parts of numbers, and are of various kinds; as, Vulgar, Decimal, Duodecimal, &c.

By fractional numbers, most questions may be solved as well as by whole numbers, and many operations more precisely performed.

Rules and Maxims for Boys at School.

YE docile youths, who learning love,
And would in various arts improve,
And to be taught to me repair,
These precepts in your memory bear:
When morning first unseals your eyes,
And bids you to your labours rise,
To God with pious ardour pray,
That he would bless your following day.
For all your studies are but vain,
Which no celestial blessing gain.
When wash'd and decent in your dress,
Let each in school assume his place,
And while you at your books remain,
Let awful silence ever reign:
For stillness I have found by use,
Will to your progress much conduce;
All chat and play are here debarr'd,
No voice but his that says, is heard;
And whatsoever task's assign'd,
Perform it with a willing mind.

You that in writing would excel,
First imitate your copies well:
Down strokes make strong, and upward fine,
And boldness with your freedom join.
If by luxuriant fancy bent,
You aim at curious ornament,
Your plastic pen, by frequent use,
May fishes, beasts, and birds produce:
But chiefly strive to gain a hand
For business, with a just command.
When figures exercise your quill,
They ask your care and all your skill;
Your fancy may in writing guide,
But reason here must be applied.
As you the learned track pursue,
Fresh useful scenes will crowd your view;
The mathematics' spacious field
Will grand and noble prospects yield;
Whether by maps o'er seas you rove,
Or trace the starry globes above,
What rapturous pleasures will you find,
When demonstration feasts the mind!

Abominate a lying tongue,
And never do your fellow wrong;
From oaths and idle talk refrain,
And old wives' fables, for they're vain.
But if sometimes you be inclin'd
To give refreshment to the mind,
Historians and poetic lays,
At once will both instruct and please.
But wanton song and wild romance,
Be ever banish'd far from hence.
Soon as your judgment waxes strong,
And can distinguish right and wrong,
Think it no task to read in youth
The Testament of sacred truth;
With diligence peruse them through,
In every language that you know;
By day revolve them with delight,
And meditate therein by night

PART III.

Containing a select Collection of Words, of two, three, and four Syllaoles accented, explained, and divided into three distinct Classes, for the mor ready and easy understanding of the three principal parts of speech viz. Substantives, Adjectives, *and* Verbs; *being a useful Pocket Com panion for such as would understand what they read and write*

TABLE I.

NOUNS SUBSTANTIVE of two Syllables, accented and explained.

The accents are the same till altered by a dash (′) on the contrary Syllables.

A′b-bess, the governess of an abbey
Ab-bey, a monastery
Ab-bot, the governor of an abbey [count
Ab-stract, a short ac-
Ac-cent, the tone of the voice [proach
Ac-céss, admission, ap-
Ac-cord, agreement
Ac-count, esteem, reckoning [ing
Ac-compts, book-keep-
A′c-tor, a performer
Ad-der, a serpent
Ad-dréss, application
A′n-chor, an iron instrument for a ship
An-gel, a spirit
An-gle, a corner [icles
An-nals, yearly chron-
An-them, a divine song
An-vil, a smith's iron
As-pect, countenance
Ba-bóon, a kind of monkey
Bád-ger, a beast
Ban-ker, a trader in money
Bank-rupt, a broken person
Ban-ner, a standard or ensign [tizes
Bap-tist, one who bap-
Bar-on, a nobleman
Bed-lam, a hospital for lunatics
Bea-ver, an amphibious animal [person
Big-ot, a superstitious
Bil-let, a ticket
Bil-low, a wave swollen
Bish-op, the spiritual head of a diocese
Bit-tern, a bird so called [for a bed
Blan-ket, a covering
Blem-ish, a spot, disgrace [der
Blis-ter, a watery blad-
Blos-som, a flower
Bon-net, a sort of cap
Bor-der, an edge
Bor-ough, a town corporate
Bot-tom, the underside
Boun-ty, generosity
Bow-els, the intestines
Bride-groom, a newly married man
Bride-well, a house of correction
Brim-stone, a mineral
Buck-et, a vessel to draw water [armour
Buck-ler, a piece of
Buck-ram, stiff cloth
Budg-et, a bag
Buf-fóon, a jester
Búl-wark, a strong fo
Bur-then, a load
Bus-tard, a wild turkey
But-ler, a house steward [pilla.
But-tress, a prop o
Buz-zard, a species o hawk
Ca-bál, a private junto
Cáb-bage, a plant
Ca-bin, the chief room
Ca-ble, a rope [in a ship
Ca-dence, a fall of the voice [riot
Ca-lásh, an open cha-
Cám-phire, a kind of resin [river
Ca-nál, an artificial
Cán-cer, a virulent sore
Can-dour, sincerity
Ca-nóe, an Indian boat
Cán-non, a great gun
Can-on, an ecclesiastical law
Can-vass, coarse cloth
Ca-pers, an acid pickle
Ca-price, humour
Cár-bine, a short gun
Car-cass, a dead body
Ca-réer, a race, a course
Cár-go, the loading of a ship

Car-pet, a floor-cloth
Cas-cáde, a waterfall
Cáse-ment, a sort of window [garment
Cas-sock, a priest's
Cas-tle, a house of defence
Cau-dle, a sweet liquor
Cav-ern, a cave or den
Cause-way, a raised passage [point
Cen-tre, the middle
Cen-try, a centinel
Chal-ice, a communion cup [worship
Chap-el, a place of
Chap-ter, a division
Char-ter, a grant
Chat-tels, goods
Chest-nut, a fruit
Chil-blain, a sore swelling [tool
Chis-el, a carpenter's
Cho-rus, a concert
Cin-ders, burnt coals, ashes
Cir-cle, a round figure
Cis-tern, a vessel for water
Cit-ron, a kind of lemon
Clam-our, noise
Clar-et, a red wine
Cli-ent, one who employs a lawyer
Cli-mate, space, tract of land [house
Clois-ter, a religious
Clos-et, a small room
Clo-ver, a sort of grass
Clus-ter, a bunch
Cob-bler, a bungler
Cod-ling, an apple [ry
Cof-fee, an Indian ber-
Cof-fer, a chest or trunk [dead
Cof-fin, a chest for the
Coin-age, the making of money [learning
Col-lege, a place for
Co-lon, a stop marked thus (:)
Com-et, a blazing star
Com-merce, trade
Com-pact, agreement
Com-pass, a circle, a space [nation
Con-céit, fancy, imagi-
Cón-cord, agreement
Con-fines, bounds, limits
Con-flict, a combat
Con-flux, a flowing together
Con-gress, a meeting
Con-quest, a victory
Con-sént, agreement
Cón-sort, a companion
Con-tact, a touch, close union [house
Con-vent, a religious
Con-vex, a spherical body
Cop-per, a large boiler
Co-quétte, an amorous girl
Có-ral, a red stone
Cor-net, an ensign
Cor-nice, a moulding
Cor-sair, a sea robber
Cot-ton, woolly stuff
Cov-ert, a shelter, a thicket [wife
Coun-tess, an earl's
Coun-try, a kingdom
Cour-age, valour
Cou-ránt, a quick dance
Ców-ard, a poltroon
Cox-comb, a conceited fellow
Cred-it, reputation
Crit-ic, a nice censurer
Crys-tal, a precious stone [tenths
Cu-bit, one foot six
Cudg-el, a staff
Cul-ture, husbandry
Cu-pid, the god of love
Cu-rate, an inferior priest
Cur-rent, a running stream
Cut-ler, a knife-maker, &c. [philosopher
Cyn-ic, a snarling
Cy-press, a tree so called
Dag-ger, a short sword
Dam-ask, flowered silk, &c
Dan-ger, hazard
Dar-nel, a weed so called
Das-tard, a coward
Dea-con, a minister
De-báte, a dispute
Débt-or, one who owes money
De-céit, a deception
De-cree, an order
De-fault, a want, an omission
De-fect, a blemish
De-fence, a resistance
De-gree, an advancement
Dé-ism, a denying of revealed religion
De-light, joy
Dél-uge, a flood
De-scént, a going down
De-sign, an invention
De-spite, envy
De-tail, the particulars
Di-et, food, an assembly [dislike
Dis-gúst, a distaste or
Dól-lar, a foreign coin
Do-lour, grief, pain
Dol-phin, a sea-fish
Do-tage, excessive fondness [twelve
Doz-en, the number
Dra-per, one who sells cloth [mour
Drop-sy, a watery hu-
Drudg-er, a mean labourer
Drug-get, woollen stuff
Drug-gist, a dealer in drugs
Du-el, a single combat
Ea-gle, a bird so called
Ease-ment, a refreshing
Ec-ho, the resounding of a voice
E-clipse, a defect of light
E'-dict, a proclamation
Ef-fécts, goods
E'-gress, a going forth

En-gine, an instrument
En-voy, a messenger
En-vy, spite
Er-rand, a message
Es-sence, substance or being [clusion
E-vént, an end or con-
Ex'-ile, banishment
Ex-it, a departure
Ex-pánse, the firmament
Ex-pense, cost, charge
Ex-ploit, an achievment
Ex-tent, compass
Fáb-ric, a building
Far-thing, the 1-4th of a penny [six feet
Fath om, a measure of
Fa-tigue, weariness
Fig-ure, a number, an image [relish
Fla-vour, a taste or
Flem-ing, a native of Flanders
Flex-ure, a bending
Flor-ist, one skilled in flowers [body
Flu-id, a thin flowing
For-est, a wild woody tract of land [er
For-ger, a counterfeit-
For-tress, a fortified place
Foun-tain, a spring
Frac-ture, a breach
Frag-ment, a broken piece
Fren-zy, madness
Fri-day, the sixth day of the week
Frig-ate, a small ship
Frol-ic, a merry prank
Fur-nace, an inclosed fire-place
Fur-row, a trench
Gal-lon, a measure of four quarts [music
Gam-ut, a scale of
Gan-grene, a mortification
Gar-ment, a coat [room
Gar-ret, an uppermost
Gaug-ing, measuring casks
Ga-zétte, a newspaper
Ghér-kins, pickled cucumbers [person
Gi-ant, a very large
Gib-bet, a gallows [2s.
Guil-der, a coin value
Glut-ton, a greedy eater [ment
Gos-pel, the New Testa-
Gos-sip, a tattling woman
Gram-mar, a book teaching to speak and write correctly
Gran-deur, greatness, power
Gri-máce, hypocrisy
Gris-tle, a bony substance [advice
Gui-dance, direction,
Gut-ter, a sink or drain
Hab-it, a custom, clothing [speech
Ha-rángue, a public
Hár-bour, a port, shelter
Har-lot, a prostitute
Har-ness, traces for horses
Har-vest, reaping time
Hatch-et, a small axe
Hav-oc, destruction
Hea-then, an idolater
Hei-fer, a young cow
Hel-met, a head-piece
Hem-lock, a poisonous plant
Her-ald, an officer
Her-bal, a book of plants [person
Her-mit, a solitary
Her-on, a large water fowl
Hire-ling, one who serves for wages
Hom-age, submission
Hon-our, respect
Hor-ror, dread
Hu-mour, fancy, moisture [food
Hun-ger, a want of
Hys-sop, an herb
Im-age, a picture or statue
Im-port, a meaning
Im-post, a toll or tax
Im-pulse, a strong persuasion
In-come, rent, revenue
In-dex, a hand or mark [☞] [search
In-quest, an inquiry,
In-road, an invasion
In-sect, a small living creature
In-sult, an affront
In-trigue, a plot
Jár-gon, gibberish, jangling [party
Jun-to, a faction,
Ken-nel, a water-course
Ker-nel, the inside of a nut
Ker-sey, coarse cloth
Knuc-kle, a joint
Lan-cet, a surgeon's instrument
Lan-guage, speech
Latch-et, a shoe-string
Leg-ate, an ambassador [writing
Le-gend, a fabulous
Li-bel, a defamatory writing [liberty
Li-cense, permission,
Lim-ner, a painter
Li-quid, a fluid substance [soning
Lo-gic, the art of rea-
Lu-cre, gain, profit
Lus-tre, brightness, eminence
Ma-chíne, an engine
Mág-net, a loadstone
Maid-en, a virgin
Man-date, a command
Man-tle, a cloak
Mar-gin, the brim or edge [woman
Ma-tron, a motherly
Max-im, a principle
May-or, a magistrate
Med-al, a coin
Mem-brane, a thin skin
Mer-it, worth
Mes-sage, an errand

Me-tal, gold, silver, &c.
Mim-ic, a ludicrous imitator
Min-ute, the 60th part of an hour
Mir-ror, a looking-glass
Mis-chief, hurt, harm
Mi-ser, a covetous fellow
Mi-tre, a bishop's cap
Mix-ture, a mingling
Mod-el, a representation, a copy
Mo-ment, an instant, importance
Mo-tive, inducement
Mot-to, a short sentence [high hill
Moun-tain, a large
Mu-sic, harmony
Mus-tard, a small seed
Na-tive, one born in any place
Na-ture, constitution, disposition, natural affection
Na-vel, a part of the belly
Na-vy, a fleet of ships
Ni-tre, saltpetre
Non-age, minority
Nov-el, a story [ance
Nui-sance, an annoy-
Nur-ture, food, diet
Ob-ject, that which presents itself
Ob-long, a long square
O-dour, a sweet scent or smell
O-men, a sign or token
Or-gan, a musical instrument [child
Or-phan, a fatherless
O-val, a figure like an egg [front
Out-rage, a violent af-
Pack-et, a parcel, a vessel
Pa-gan, a heathen
Paint-er, one who
Pal-ace, a court [paints
Pal-ate, the roof of the mouth
Pal-sy, a disease

Pan-ic, sudden fear
Pa-pist, a Roman catholic [write on
Parch-ment, a skin to
Pars-ley, a culinary
Pas-time, sport [herb
Pas-tor, a minister
Pa-tent, an exclusive right [fellow
Pea-sant, a country
Peb-bles, small stones
Pen-ance, an atonement
Per-fume, a sweet scent
Phan-tom, a ghost
Phœ-nix, a rare bird
Phys-ic, a medicine
Pic-kle, a preserve
Pic-ture, a representation [a ship
Pi-lot, one who steers
Pin-nace, a boat
Pi-rate, a sea robber
Pis-mire, an ant
Plain-tiff, he who complaineth
Plas-ter, or *Plais-ter*, a cover for a sore
Pre-cept, a command
Pre-cinct, a jurisdiction
Prel-áte, a bishop
Pre-lude, an introduction
Pre-ténce, an excuse
Pré-text, a pretence
Pri-mate, the chief archbishop
Prim-er, a little book
Prin-cess, a king's daughter
Prob-lem, a question
Pro-cess, a proceeding
Proc-tor, a spiritual officer [produced
Pro-duct, the thing
Pro-gress, course, circuit
Pro-ject, a contrivance
Pro-logue, an introduction to a play
Proph-et, an inspired person
Pros-pect, a view
Prox-y, a deputy

Pur-port, a meaning
Pur-pose, a design
Pur-súit, the act of following [strument
Qúad-rant, a marine in
Quar-rel, a brawl, strife [rows
Quiv-er, a case for ar-
Quo-rum, a bench of justices
Quo-ta, a share, a rate
Rab-ble, a mob
Ra-dix, the root
Rai-ment, a garment
Rai-sin, a dried grape
Ran-cour, malice
Ran-dom, uncertainty
Rap-ine, robbery
Rap-ture, a transport of mind
Rash-ness, hastiness
Ra-zor, an instrument to shave with
Re-céipt, a discharge
Re-cess, a withdrawing
Réc-ord, a register
Rec-tor, the parson of a parish
Re-flux, a flowing back
Ref-uge, a place of safety
Re-gárd, respect
Rél-ict, a widow
Re-lief, assistance
Re-nown, fame
Re-past, a meal
Rés-pite, a delay for some time
Re-súlt, a conclusion
Re-venge, satisfaction
Re-view, an examination [plant
Rhú-barb, a purging
Rid-dle, a dark saying
Rig-our, harshness, strictness
Ri-ot, tumult, noise
Ro-mánce, a feigned story
Rúb-bish, refuse, dirt
Ru-bric, the church service
Rup-ture, a breaking
Sab-bath, a day of rest

Sa-ble, a rich fur
Sa-bre, a sword
Sal-ad, food of raw herbs [of a plant
Sam-phire, the name
Sam-ple, a pattern
San-dal, a sort of shoe
Sap-phire, a costly stone
Sar-casm, a scoff or taunt
Satch-el, a bag for books
Sat-in, a sort of silk
Sat-urn, one of the planets
Scab-bard, a sheath
Scan-dal, offence, infamy
Scep-tre, a royal staff
Scep-tic, a doubter
Schol-ar, a learned person
Sci-ence, knowledge
Scoun-drel, a rascally fellow
Scrip-tures, the old and new testaments
Sci-on, a graft
Scru-ple, a doubt
Sculp-ture, carved work
Scur-vy, a disease
Seg-ment, a piece cut off
Ser-pent, a venomous creature [cer
Sex-ton, a church offi-
Sham-bles, butchers' stalls
Sharp-er, a cheat
Shek-el, a Jewish coin
Si-byls, certain prophetesses
Sig-nal, a sign or token
Sig-net, a seal set in a ring
Si-ren, a mermaid
Slov-en, a dirty fellow
Slug-gard, a slothful person [poem
Son-net, an Italian
Soph-ist, a subtle dis-
Sor-row, grief [puter
Spar-row, a bird
Spec-tre, an apparition
Spin-age, a vegetable
Spin-et', a musical instrument [woman
Spin-ster, a maiden
Splin-ter, a shiver of wood
Spon-sor, a surety
Squir-rel, a small nimble animal
Sta-tue, an image
Stat-ure, shape, size
Stat-ute, a law
Stew-ard, an overseer
Sti-pend, a salary
Stir-rup, belonging to a saddle [body
Stom-ach, a part of the
Stow-age, warehouse room
Sto-ry, a tale
Stream-er, a flag
Strip-ling, a youth
Struc-ture, a building
Stub-ble, stalks of corn
Stu-dent, one who studies
Sub-stance, wealth
Sub-urbs, the out parts of a city
Suc-cess, good luck
Suc-cour, help, assistance
Suf-frage, a vote
Sui-tor, a wooer, a petitioner
Sul-phur, brimstone
Sum-mer, the second season of the year
Sum-mit, the highest part
Sure-ty, safety, bail
Sur-face, the outside of any thing
Sur-feit, an indisposition [ment
Sur-prise, astonish-
Swal-low, a bird
Sym-bol, a badge or mark
Symp-tom, a sign or token
Syn-od an ecclesiastical assembly
Sys-tem, a scheme which unites many things in order
Ta-ble, a flat surface, an index to a book
Tai-lor, a maker of clothes [ulty
Tal-ent, a gift, a fac-
Tal-low, melted fat
Tal-on, a claw
Tank-ard, a mug with a lid [hides
Tan-ner, one who tans
Ta-per, a long wax light, &c. [liquors
Tap-ster, a drawer of
Tar-get, a shield
Tas-sel, a bunch of fringe
Tav-ern, a house where wine is sold
Tem-per, natural disposition
Tem-pest, a storm
Ten-ant, one who hires
Ten-et, a doctrine or opinion
Ten-ter, a hook
Ter-race, a bank of earth, a raised wall
Ter-ror, fright
Tes-ter, part of a bed
Tet-ter, a humour
Tex-ture, a web
Thick-et, a place full of bushes [plant
This-tle, a prickly
Thrash-er, one who thrashes [the air
Thun-der, a noise in
Thurs-day, the fifth day of the week
Tick-et, a small note
Ti-ger, a furious wild beast [building
Tim-ber, wood for
Tim-brel, a musical instrument [dye
Tinc-ture, a stain or
Tin-der, burnt rags
Tin-ker, a mender of vessels [impost
Ton-nage, a duty or
Top-ic, head of a discourse

Tor-rent, a violent stream
Tor-toise, a shell fish
Tow-er, a castle
Tow-el, a cloth to dry the hands
Traf-fic, trade, commerce
Trai-tor, one guilty of treason
Trans-cript, a copy
Tran-sit, a pass
Trav-ail, labour, pains
Trea-cle, dregs of sugar
Trea-son, disloyalty
Trea-sure, riches, goods
Trea-tise, a discourse
Tre-mour, a trembling
Trench-es, deep ditches
Tri-bune, a magistrate
Trib-ute, a tax
Troop-er, a horse soldier
Tro-phy, a sign of victory
Trow-el, a mason's tool
Trum-pet, a musical instrument
Trus-tee', a guardian
Tri-al, an examination
Tues-day, the third day of the week
Tu-lip, a flower
Tu-mour, a swelling
Tu-mult, a riot
Tun-nel, a funnel
Tur-key, a large fowl
Tur-nip, a white root
Tur-ret, a small tower
Tur-tle, the sea tortoise
Tu-tor, an instructer
Twi-light, dusk
Ty-rant, a cruel governor
Ty-ro, a novice, a beginner
Ud-der, the dug of a cow
Ul-cer, a running sore
Um-pire, an arbitrator
Un-cle, a father, or mother's brother
Ur-chin, an unlucky child
U-rine, a person's water
U-sage, custom
Ush-er, an under master
Va-grant, an idle person
Val-lance, short curtains
Val-ley, a low part
Val-our, courage
Val-ue, worth or price
Va-pour, steam
Var-let, a knave
Var-nish, a glossy paint
Vas-sal, a slave
Vel-lum, calf's skin parchment
Vel-vet, fine silk manufacture
Ven-om, poison
Ve-nus, the goddess of beauty
Ver-dict, the report of justice
Ver-dure, greenness
Ver-juice, juice of crabs
Ver-min, any noxious insect &c.
Ves-sel, a small ship,
Ves-tels, a sort of priestesses
Ves-tige, a footstep
Ves-try, a place in the church
Ves-ture, a garment
Vi-al, a small glass bottle
Vic-ar, a deputy
Vic-tim, a sacrifice
Vic-tor, a conqueror
Vig-our, strength
Vil-lage, a small town
Vil-lain, a rogue
Vint-ner, a seller of wine
Vi-per, a venomous creature
Vir-gin, a chaste maiden
Vir-tue, quality, honesty
Vis-age, countenance
Vis-count,* the next degree to an earl
Vi-sor, a mask
Vis-ta, a view
Vol-ley, a discharge of guns
Vol-ume, a complete book
Vul-can, a pagan god
Wa-fer, a thin dried paste
Wag-on, a carriage
Wains-cot, thin boards fixed to a wall
Wal-let, a travelling bag
Wal-nut, a large nut
Wal-ter, a man's name
Ward-en, a guardian
Ward-robe, a place for clothes
War-fare, military service
War-rant, a written order
War-ren, a place for rabbits
Wea-pon, an instrument of offence or defence
Wea-ther, the state of the air
Wea-ver, one who weaves
Wea-sel, a little wild animal
Wher-ry, a small boat
Wick-et, a little gate
Wid-ow, one whose husband is dead
Wil-low, a tree so called
Wood-cock, a bird well known
Wrest-ling, an exercise
Wri-ting, any thing written
Yeo-man, a freeholder
Young-ster, a young fellow
Zea-lot, a zealous person
Zen-ith, a point over head

A'b-ject, mean, base
Ab-rúpt, unseasonable
A'b-sent, not present
Ab-strúse, secret, difficult
Ab-surd, foolish,
A-cute, ingenious
A'd-junct, joined to
Ad-verse, not prosperous
A-dúlt, full grown
A'-gile, quick, nimble
A-lért, brisk
An-tique, strange, ancient
A'r-dent, zealous
Au-gúst, sacred
Bárb-ed, bearded
Be-nign, courteous
Blight-ed, blasted
Boor-ish, clownish
Bra-ced, joined together
Braw-ny, sinewy, lusty
Bru-mal, belonging to winter
Bul-bous, having round roots
Bul-ky, big, lusty
Cal-lous, hard, unfeeling
Cal-low, unfledged
Can-did, sincere
Car-nal, fleshly
Caus-tic, searing, burning
Child-ish, simple, trifling
Ci-vil, courteous
Clev-er, nice, ingenious
Clot-ted, in lumps
Com-plex, difficult
Con-cave, hollow
Con-cise, short
Con-dign, deserved
Cón-trite, penitent
Cor-réct, without fault
Cós-tive, bound in body
Craf-ty, cunning
Dain-ty, nice in diet
De-cent, becoming
De-múre, over grave
De-vout, godly
Dire-ful, terrible, cursed
Dis-júnct, disjointed
Di-vers, sundry, several
Di-vérse, different
Di-vine, heavenly
Dóle-ful, mournful
Dor-mant, sleeping, inactive
Drow-sy, sleepy, heavy
Duc-tile, apt to draw out
Ea-ger, earnest
Earn-est, steadfast
En-ti're, whole
E'p-ic, heroic
E-qual, even
Ex-áct, nice, curious
Ex-empt, free from
Ex-pert, cunning
Ex-tinct, put out, dead
Fá-cile, easy to be done
Fee-ble, weak
Fer-tile, fruitful
Fic-kle, given to change
Fi-nite, that which has an end
Fla-grant, manifest
Fledg-ed, covered with feathers
Flor-id, blooming, embellished
Flu-ent, eloquent in speech
For-eign, outlandish
For-lórn, helpless, forsaken
Fór-mal, affected
Fra-grant, of a sweet smell
Fri-gid, cold
Fru-gal, thrifty
Fu-ture, yet to come
Gal-lant, brave, genteel
Gau-dy, fine, gay
Gen-téel, neat, fine, gallant
Gén-tle, civil, mild, tame
Gid-dy, wild, inconsiderate
Hand some, comely
Haugh-ty, proud
Hea-dy, strong, unruly
Hec-tic, consumptive
Hei-nous, very wicked
Hon-est, just
Hor-rid, dreadful
Hos-tile, war-like, adverse
Hu-máne, courteous, very kind
Húm-ble, modest
Hu-mid, moist
Im-ménse, exceedingly great
In-firm, weak
In-nate, inbred
Kná-vish, deceitful, cheating
Lan-guid, weak, faint
La-tent, lying hid
Lim-pid, clear
Lo-cal, belonging to a place
Lof-ty, high
Lu-cid, bright
Lyr-ic, belonging to the harp
Ma-gic, black, devilish
Maim-ed, hurt
Ma-túre, perfect
Migh-ty, powerful
Mi-núte, small
Mod-ern, new
Mo-dish, fashionable
Mon-strous, prodigious
Mor-al, belonging to manners
Mun-dane, worldly
Ner-vous, sinewy
Neth-er, lower
Neu-ter, of neither side
Ni-trous, consisting of nitre
No-cent, hurtful
Noi-some, loathsome
Ob-lique, crooked
Ob-scene, filthy, rude
Ob-scure, dark
Ob-tuse, blunt
Oc-cult, secret hidden

Pál-try, pitiful, mean
Pa-pal, belonging to the pope [meek
Pas-sive, submissive,
Pa-tent, open, appropriated by license
Peev-ish, fretful
Pen-sive, melancholy, thoughtful
Per-vérse, obstinate
Plú-ral, comprising more than one
Po-lite, neat, genteel
Pó-tent, powerful
Pre-cise, formal, exact
Prég-nant, breeding, fruitful
Pris-tine, ancient
Pri-vate, hid
Pro-fáne, wicked
Pro-fuse, lavish
Pro-lix, long, tedious
Pu-trid, corrupt
Ram-pant, wanton
Rap-id, swift
Re-cent, new
Re-gal, kingly
Re-miss, negligent
Re-mote, foreign, distant
Rig-id, severe [tant
Ro-búst, lusty, strong
Ró-guish, knavish
Roy-al, kingly
Rud-dy, somewhat red
Ru-ral, like the country
Rus-tic, rude, plain, artless
Sa-ble, black, dark
Sa-cred, holy
San-guine, murderous, bloody
Sav-age, brutish
Sau-cy, unmannerly, rude [red colour
Scar-let, of a bright
Se-cret, concealed, private [danger
Se-cúre, safe, free from
Se-date, quiet
Se-lect, choice
Se-rene, clear, calm
Sér-vile, mean, base
Shal-low, empty
Shame-less, impudent
Shame-fáced, bashful
Sick-ly, unhealthy
Sim-ple, pure, unmixed, foolish
Sin-cére, honest
Skit-tish, wanton
Slen-der, thin, slight, weak
Smut-ty, filthy
So-lar, belonging to the sun [reverence
So-lemn, done with
Sol-id, firm, everlasting
Sol-vent, able to pay
Sor-did, mean, base
Spee-dy, quick, nimble
Splen-did, glorious
Spright-ly, brisk, lively
Spun-gy, full of holes
Squal-id, foul, nasty
Squeam-ish, nice, fastidious [still
Stag-nant, standing
State-ly, majestic
Stea-dy, even, firm
Stel-lar, starry
Ster-il, unfruitful
Stub-born, obstinate
Stu-pid, dull, senseless
Stur-dy, resolute
Sub-lime, high, lofty
Súb-tile, crafty, thin, fine
Suc-cinct, brief, short
Súd-den, hasty, quick
Sul-len, gloomy
Sul-try, very hot
Sun-dry, several, many
Su-pine, careless
Súp-ple, tender, pliant
Su-préme, highest
Swár-thy, tawney, blackish
Syl-van, relating to woods
Ta-cit, silent, implied, not expressed
Taint-ed, corrupted
Tar-dy, dull, slow, guilty
Taunt-ing, scoffing
Taw-dry, foolishly gay
Taw-ny, brownish
Tes-ty, peevish, churlish
Tin-ged, coloured [ish
Tor-pid, benumbed, sleepy
Tor-rid, hot, burning
To-tal, entire, whole
To-ward, froward, apt
Trans-verse, across, athwart [fearful
Trep-id, trembling,
Tri-ple, threefold, treble [est, true
Trus-ty, faithful, hon-
Tu-mid, swelled, puffed up [bloated
Tur-gid, swollen,
Un-couth, awkward, strange
Un-wise, foolish, weak
Up-right, sincere, honest [polite
Ur-báne, courteous,
Vá-cant, void, empty, free
Vap-id, dead, flat
Ver-bal, by word of mouth [ishing
Ver-dant, green, flour-
Ver-nal, belonging to spring
Vi-nous, having the quality of wine
Vis-cous, clammy, glutinous [life
Vi-tal, belonging to
Viv-id, lively, sprightly [the voice
Vo-cal, belonging to
Vo-lant, flying, quick, active [mean, low
Vul-gar, common,
Wan-ton, licentious, loose
Weal-thy, rich, opulent
Weigh-ty, heavy, important
Wo-ful, sorrowful, sad
Wool-len, made of wool
Year-ly, annual
Yes-ty, spungy, barmy
Youth-ful, young, juvenile
Zea-lous, ardent, eager
Zig-zag, winding, spiral

TABLE III.

VERBS OF TWO SYLLABLES, ACCENTED AND EXPLAINED.

A-ba'se, to bring down, to humble
A-bate, to diminish
A-bet, to encourage, to aid, humble
A-bide, to continue, to dwell [upon oath
Ab-jure, to renounce
A-bridge, to shorten, to diminish [self
Ab-scond, to hide one's
Ab-sorb, to swallow up
Ab-stain, to forbear, to cease [to cleanse
Ab-sterge, to purge,
Ab-stract, to separate
Ac-cost, to address, to salute
Ac-crue, to arise from
Ac-cuse, to charge with guilt
Ac-quit, to discharge
Ad-dict, to accustom, to devote
Ad-here, to cleave to
Ad-journ, to put off, to defer
A-dopt, to take in the place of a child
A-dorn, to beautify
Ad-vert, to attend to
Af-firm, to maintain
Af-fix, to subjoin
Al-lay, to assuage, to pacify [declare
Al-lege, to affirm, to
Al-lure, to decoy, to entice
A-mass, to heap up
A-maze, to surprise, to terrify [fine
A-merse, to inflict a
An-nex, to join together [bull
Be'l-low, to roar like a
Be-móan, to lament, to bewail [will
Be-queath, to give by
Be-reave, to deprive of
Be-wail, to lament

Bi-sect, to cut into two equal parts
Blá-zon, to adorn, to display [trust
Bor-row, to take upon
Bran-dish, to flourish, to wave
Bun-gle, to botch
Bur-nish, to polish, to make bright
Ca-jo'le, to flatter, to deceive [calx
Cál-cine, to burn to a
Can-cel, to blot out, to erase [fondness
Ca-réss, to treat with
Ca-rouse, to drink hard
Ca's-trate, to geld
Ce-mént, to unite, to join, to solder
Cén-sure, to blame, to condemn [combat
Chal-lenge, to call to
Chas-tise, to correct, to punish [to name
Chris-ten, to baptize,
Clat-ter, to make a noise [gether
Co-hére, to stick to-
Col-lect, to gather together [duel
Com-bat, to fight a
Com-bine, to join together
Com-mend, to praise
Com-mit, to imprison, to intrust [course
Com-mune, to dis-
Com-pare, to liken
Co'm-pass, to surround, to grasp [constrain
Com-pél, to force, to
Com-pile, to collect
Com-plain, to murmur
Com-plete, to perfect, to finish [together
Com-plore, to lament
Com-port, to behave
Com-pose, to put together

Com-pound, to mix together [close
Com-press, to squeeze
Com-prise, to contain
Com-pute, to reckon
Con-ceal, to keep secret
Con-cede, to yield, to admit
Con-cert, to contrive
Con-clude, to finish
Con-cur, to agree with
Con-demn, to find guilty
Con-dense, to thicken
Con-dole, to lamen with
Con-duce, to promote
Con-fer, to bestow, compare
Con-fide, to trust in
Con-fine, to restrain
Con-firm, to establish
Con-form, to compl with
Con-found, to puzzle
Con-front, to oppose
Con-fuse, to perplex
Con-fute, to disprove
Con-geal, to harden
Con-join, to put together
Cón-jure, to practis enchantment
Con-júre, to enjoin solemnly
Con-nect, to join
Con-nive, to wink at a fault [fruit
Con-serve, to preserve
Con-sign, to deliver up
Con-spire, to plot
Co'n-strue, to expound
Con-súlt, to advise
Con-sume, to waste
Con-temn, to despise
Con-tend, to quarrel to strive
Con-test, to dispute
Con-tract, to bargain for

Con-trive, to invent
Con-trol, to restrain
Con-vene, to assemble
Con-verse, to talk together
Con-vert, to change
Con-vey, to make over
Con-vict, to prove guilty
Con-voke, to call together
Con-voy, to conduct
Cor-rect, to chastise
Cor-rode, to fret or gnaw
Cor-rupt, to debauch
Cóv-et, to desire
Cou-ple, to join together
Coz-en, to cheat
Cur-táil, to abridge, to cut short
Dáb-ble, to paddle in water
Dal-ly, to sport with
Dam-age, to hurt
De-bár, to exclude, to hinder
De-base, to bring down
De-bate, to dispute
De-bauch, to corrupt
De-cant, to pour off
De-cay, to grow worse
De-cease, to die
De-cede, to part from
De-cide, to conclude a matter
De-claim, to speak against
De-cline, to refuse
De-coy, to entice
De-cry, to speak ill of
De-feat, to overthrow
De-fend, to support, to protect or guard
De-fer, to put off
De-fine, to exclaim
De-flour, to ravish
De-form, to disfigure
De-fraud, to cheat
De-fray, to bear expenses
De-fy, to challenge
De-grade, to lessen, to disgrace
De-ject, to cast down
De-lay, to put off
De-lude, to deceive
De-mand, to lay claim to
De-mean, to debase
De-merge, to plunge down
De-mise, to bequeath
De-mur, to object, to hesitate
De-note, to point out, to show
De-nounce, to proclaim, to declare
De-part, to go from
De-pend, to rely upon
De-plore, to bewail
De-plume, to unfeather
De-port, to behave one's self
De-pose, to dethrone, to witness
De-prave, to corrupt
De-press, to weigh down
De-pute, to empower, to act
Des-cry, to discern afar off
De-sign, to intend, to purpose
De-sist, to leave off
De-spoil, to strip, to rob
De-spond, to despair
De-tach, to separate
De-ter, to affright, to stop
De-tect, to discover
De-test, to abhor
De-tract, to take from
De-vote, to dedicate
Dic-tate, to give orders
Dif-fúse, to spread abroad
Di-gest, to set in order
Di-gress, to deviate, to err
Di-late, to widen
Di-lute, to make thin
Dis-arm, to divest of arms, to foil
Dis-burse, to lay out money
Dis-card, to discharge
Dis-cern, to perceive
Dis-claim, to disown
Dis-close, to discover
Dis-own, to deny
Dis-pel, to drive away
Dis-pense, to excuse, to deal out
Dis-play, to unfold
Dis-sect, to cut open
Dis-sent, to disagree
Dis-taste, to dislike
Dis-suade, to divert
Dis-tend, to stretch out
Dis-til, to drop down
Dis-tort, to wrest aside
Dis-use, to forbare to use
Di-vert, to turn aside from
Di-vest, to strip, to dispossess
Di-vorce, to put away
Di-vulge, to spread abroad
Dwin-dle, to waste away
E-clipse, to darken
Ef-face, to destroy
Ef-fect, to perform
E-ject, to cast out
E-late, to puff up
E-lect, to choose, to appoint
E-lude, to shift, to shun
Em-balm, to preserve a corpse
Em-bark, to go on shipboard
E-merge, to issue, to rise out of
E-mit, to send forth
E-mulge, to milk out
En-act, to decree
En-chant, to bewitch, to delight
En-close, to include
En-dear, to make beloved
En-dure, to undergo, to bear
En-force, to constrain
En-gage, to persuade, to fight
En-graft, to inoculate trees
En-gross, to monopolize
En-hance, to raise the value
En-rol, to register, to record
En-tail, to make over
En-tice, to attempt

E-quip, to furnish
E-rase, to blot out
E-rect, to build
Es-say, to attempt, to undertake [put off
E-vade, to shun, to
E-vince, to prove
Ex-alt, to lift up
Ex-cite, to stir up
Ex-ert, to put forth
Ex-hale, to breathe, to evaporate [consume
Ex-haust, to empty, to
Ex-ist, to have being
Ex-pand, to spread, to diffuse
Ex-pel, to drive out
Ex-pend, to lay out, to disburse
Ex-pire, to close, to die
Ex-plore, to decry, to reject
Ex-port, to send abroad
Ex-punge, to blot out
Ex-tol, to celebrate, to praise [force
Ex-tort, to gain by
Ex-trude, to push, or thrust off
Ex-ult, to leap for joy
Fám-ish, to starve
Fer-mént, to swell, to puff up [falsely
Flát-ter, to praise
Flour-ish, to prosper, to thrive [encourage
Fo-mént, to bathe, to
Fór-feit, to lose by neglect [point
Frus-trate, to disap-
Fur-bish, to brighten
Gar-nish, to adorn
Glit-ter, to shine, to sparkle
Hal-low, to make holy
Hal-lóo, to set on, or incite a dog
Hár-row, to break clods
Haz-ard, to venture
Ho-ver, to flutter
Il-lúde to mock, to deceive
Im-bibe, to suck in, to receive

Im-brue, to wet, to steep, to soak
Im-merge, } to dip
Im-merse, }
Im-part, to disclose
Im-pede, to hinder, to stop
Im-peach, to accuse
Im-pel, to urge or drive forward
Im-pend, to hang over, to await
Im-plore, to beseech
Im-ply, to contain, to signify [mind
Im-print, to fix in the
Im-pute, to ascribe
In-cite, to stir up
In-clude, to comprehend
In-cur, to fall under
In-dent, to cut on the edges
In-dict, to accuse
In-dite, to dictate
In-dorse, to write on the back [taint
In-fect, to corrupt, to
In-ject, to cast in
In-sert, to place among other things
In-spect, to look into
In-spire, to breathe into
In-stil, to infuse
In-sure, to exempt from
In-trude, to encroach
In-veigh, to rail against
In-vert, to turn upside down
In-vest, to put in possession [fold in
In-volve, to wrap, to
In-ure, to accustom
Lá-bour, to take pains
Lan-guish, to pine away
Main-táin, to uphold
Mán-age, to husband, to do well
Man-gle, to rend or cut
Ma-núre, to dung, to enrich

Már-vel, to wonder
Mo-lést, to disturb
Múr-der, to kill
Muz-zle, to tie up the mouth
Neg-lèct, to disregard
Núr-ture, to train up to educate
Nour-ish, to maintain
Num-ber, to count, to reckon
O-béy, to submit
Ob-trude, to thrust in, to impose
Oc-cur, to appear
O-mit, to leave out, to neglect
Op-pose, to withstand
Op-press, to injure, to subdue
Op-pugn, to resist
Or-dain, to appoint
Pár-boil, to boil only in part
Par-ley, to talk with
Par-táke, to take part with
Pèr-ish, to decay, to die
Per-jure, to forswear, to take a false oath
Per-mit, to allow
Per-plex, to distract
Per-sist, to persevere
Per-suade, to make believe
Per-tain, to belong
Per-vert, to seduce
Pe-ruse, to read over
Pic-kle, to preserve
Pil-fer, to steal
Pil-lage, to plunder
Plun-der, to rob
Pol-ish, to make bright
Pon-der, to consider
Por-ténd, to betoken
Por-tray, to pain truly
Post-pone, to put off
Pre-cede, to go before
Pre-dict, to foretell
Pre-fix, to set before
Pre-mise, to treat before
Pre-sage, to forebode

Pre-scribe, to appoint
Pre-sent, to give
Pre-side, to rule over
Pro-claim, to declare, to tell
Pro-duce, to bring forth
Pro-mote, to advance
Pro-long, to lengthen
Pro-mulge, to publish, to proclaim
Pro-nounce, to utter
Pro-pound, to propose
Pro-rogue, to put off, to prolong
Pro-tect, to defend
Pro-tend, to stretch out
Pro-trude, to thrust forward
Púz-zle, to confound
Quib-ble, to equivocate
Quick-en, to hasten
Ral-ly, to banter, to chide
Ram-ble, to go astray
Ran-sack, to rifle
Ran-som, to redeem
Re-búke, to reprove
Re-call, to call back
Re-cant, to retract an opinion
Re-cede, to depart from
Re-cite, to rehearse
Re-claim, to amend
Re-cline, to lean backwards
Re-close, to close again
Re-coil, to fly back
Re-count, to relate
Re-cruit, to supply
Re-cur, to return
Re-deem, to recover
Re-dound, to conduce
Re-dress, to reform
Re-duce, to subdue, to bring back [refute
Re-fel, to disprove, to
Re-fer, to direct, to submit
Re-fine, to purify
Re-fit, to fit out again
Re-flect, to think seriously
Re-form, to amend
Re-frain, to forbear

Re-fresh, to revive
Re-fund, to pay back
Re-fute, to disprove
Re-gain, to get again
Re-gret, to be sorry for
Re-hearse, to relate
Re-ject, to cast off, to despise
Re-join, to reply
Re-lapse, to fall into again [cite
Re-late, to tell, to re-
Re-lax, to slacken, to remit [sion
Re-lent, to feel compas-
Rél-ish, to taste, to approve [tice
Re-márk, to take no-
Re-mit, to pay, to forgive [afresh
Re-new, to begin
Re-pair, to amend
Re-peal, to make void
Re-peat, to say over again
Re-pel, to drive back
Re-pine, to grudge, to be sorry
Re-pose, to rest
Re-press, to restrain
Re-pute, to esteem
Re-quite, to reward
Rés-cue, to deliver
Re-sént, to be angry with
Re-serve, to lay up
Re-side, to abide
Re-sign, to yield, to give up
Re-sist, to withstand
Re-sort, to repair unto
Re-spire, to breathe
Re-spond, to answer
Re-strain, to keep back
Re-tail, to sell in small quantities
Re-tain, to keep
Re-tard, to keep back, to hinder
Re-tire, to withdraw
Re-tort, to twist, to turn back
Re-tract, to draw back
Re-treat, to go away

Re-trieve, to recover
Re-veal, to discover
Re-vere, to honour
Re-verse, to repeal
Re-vert, to return
Re-vile, to reproach
Re-vise, to look over again
Re-vive, to recover
Re-voke, to call back again
Re-volt, to rebel
Re-vólve, to meditate on [pense
Re-ward, to recom-
Sa-lute, to greet, to kiss
Sau'n-ter, to loiter, to idle
Scam-per, to run away
Scat-ter, to disperse
Scrib-ble, to write badly
Se-clúde, to shut out
Se-duce, to mislead
Sév-er, to part asunder
Shad-ow, to screen
Shat-ter, to break into pieces
Show-er, to pour down
Shud-der, to quake, to tremble
Shuf-fle, to shift
Slum-ber, to sleep, to doze [suffocate
Smoth-er, to choke, to
Smug-gle, to get by stealth [cheer
So-lace, to comfort, to
Spar-kle, to glitter, to shine
Spat-ter, to sprinkle
Sprin-kle, to wet with drops [stifle
Stran-gle, to choke, to
Stam-mer, to stutter
Stum-ble, to trip up in walking
Sub-dúe, to conquer
Sub-ject, to submit
Sub-join, to add to
Sub-mit, to yield, to refer to
Sub-scribe, to assign, to attest

Sub-serve, to second, to help
Sub-side, to sink down
Sub-sist, to exist, to continue
Sub-vert, to overthrow
Suc-ceed, to follow, to prosper [mind
Sug-gest, to put in
Súm-mon, to call by authority [mine
Sup-plánt, to under-
Sup-port, to uphold
Sup-pose, to imagine
Sur-charge, to overload
Sur-mise, to suspect
Sur-mount, to overcome
Sur-pass, to excel, to exceed
Sur-vey, to overlook, to measure
Sur-vive, to outlive
Sus-pend, to delay, to put off
Swád-dle, to swathe
Swag-ger, to hector, to boast
Tar-nish, to sully
Threat-en, to denounce evil
Tin-gle, to feel a sharp pain
Tor-ment, to put in pain [to tease
Tor-ture, to distress,
Tra-dúce, to slander, to accuse
Trám-ple, to tread upon
Trans-áct, to manage
Tran-scend, to surpass, to excel
Tran-scribe, to copy out
Trans-fer, to remove
Trans-form, to metamorphose
Trans-gress, to trespass
Trans-late, to interpret
Trans-mit, to convey
Trans-pierce, to run through
Trans-plant, to remove
Trans-port, to convey
Trans-pose, to displace
Tráv-el, to go a journey
Tra-verse, to cross, to travel over
Trem-ble, to shake with fear
Tre-pán, to ensnare
Trés-pass, to sin, to offend [idle
Tru-ant, to loiter, to
Trun-dle, to roll along
Tum-ble, to fall
Twin-kle, to sparkle
Twit-ter, to shake, to tremble
Up-bráid, to reproach
Up-hold, to keep up, to support [to speak
U't-ter, to pronounce,
Van-ish, to disappear
Va-pour, to brag, to bully, steam [change
Va-ry, to alter, to
Ven-ture, to hazard
Vi-brate to shake to and fro [person
Vis-it, to go to see a
Vouch-sáfe, to condescend [a duck
Wád-dle, to walk like
Wal-low, to roll in mire
Wan-der, to rove, to ramble
War-ble, to sing as birds [kindly
Wel-come, to receive
White-wash, to make white [open
Wi-den, to extend, to
With-er, to fade
Wor-ry, to tease, to tear [to fold
Wrin-kle, to crease,

TABLE IV.

NOUNS SUBSTANTIVE, OF THREE SYLLABLES, ACCENTED AND EXPLAINED.

Abéttor, one who aids
Abridgement, an epitome
A'ccidence, a little book of the first rudiments of grammar
Accident, chance, misfortune
Accómplice, a companion
Achievement, an escutcheon
Acquittal, a discharge
Adjournment, a putting off
A'djument, help, aid
Adjutant, an assistant
Admiral, a naval commander
Advénture, a chance
A'dvocate, a pleader
Affi'ance, to betroth
A'ffluence, wealth, plenty
Aggregate, the whole, the total
Aggréssor, an assaulter
A'gony, violent pain
Alderman, a magistrate
Alémbic, a distilling vessel
A'lgebra, literal arithmetic
Alien, a foreigner
Aliment, food, nourishment
Alli'ance, a league
Allotment, a part or share

A'lmanac, a yearly account of time, weather, &c.
Allówance, maintenance
A'lmoner, a disposer of alms
Alphabet, the letters of any [language
Altitude, height
Améndment, a reformation
A'mnesty, a general pardon
Amulet, a charm, a spell
Anarchy, want of government
Anchoret, a hermit
Animal, any living creature
Annóyance, damage, nuisance
A'ntidote, a remedy for poison
Aperture, an opening
Apóstate, a backslider
Apartment, a lodging
Appendage, an addition
Appendix, a supplement
A'ptitude, fitness, disposition
Aqueduct, a conduit or pipe
Arcánum, a secret, or nostrum
A'rchitect, a chief builder
Argument, reason or proof
Armáda, a great navy
A'rtery, a blood-vessel
Article, a term, a condition
Artifice, a trick, fraud, deceit
Assáilant, one who assaults
Assessor, one who rates taxes
A'theism, the denying of a God
Attribute, a property
Audience, a hearing
Avenue, a walk, a passage
Augury, a divination by birds
Auróra, poetically the morning
A'xiom, a self-evident principle
Bacchanals, drunken feast
Bachelor, an unmarried man
Baronet, one below a baron
Barrister, a lawyer
Basilisk, a serpent, a cannon
Benefice, a church living
Bigotry, superstition
Bisséxtile, leap-year
Blásphemy, indignity offered to God
Botanist, one skilled in plants
Bravery, courage
Brevity, shortness
Butterfly, a beautiful insect
Cabinet, a small chest
Calendar, an almanac
Calenture, a burning fever
Calomel, a preparation of mer- [cury
Calumny, reproach
Candidate, a competitor
Cannibal, a man-eater
Canopy, a cloth of state
Caravan, a large carriage
Cárdinal, a priest of Rome
Carpenter, an artificer in wood
Cartilage, a gristly substance
Catalogue, a list of names
Catechism, instruction in reli- [gion
Cavalry, horse soldiers
Cavalcade, a procession on [horseback
Caveat, a caution
Cavity, a hollowness
Century, an hundred years
Champion, a hero, a warrior
Chancellor, an officer of state
Chastity, purity of body
Chiméra, a wild fancy
Chrónicle, a history of events
Cinnamon, a spice
Circuit, a compass about
Citadel, a fortress, a castle
Citizen, a freeman of a city
Cognizance, judicial notice
Colloquy, a conference
Combatant, a champion
Comedy, a play
Committee, a select company
Cómplement, the full number
Compliment, an act of civility
Compósure, sedateness
Comptroller, an inspector
Concernment, an affair, business

Concurrence, union
Cónference, a formal discourse
Confluence, a concourse
Confórmist, one who conforms
Conjecture, a supposition
Connivance, a winking at
Cónsequence, an effect, a result
Contéxture, a joining together
Cóntinence, chastity
Continent, land not separated by the sea
Convéyance, the act of removing
Córoner, an officer, an enquirer
Coverture, a covering, a shelter
Courtesy, civility, kindness
Criticism, censure, remark
Crucifix, a figure of Christ on the cross
Crudity, rawness
Cucumber, a summer fruit
Custody, imprisonment
Customer, one who buys
Cylinder, a roller
Daffodil, a flower
Dalliance, fondness, pastime
Debauchée, a drunkard, a rake
Debénture, a writ
Decanter, a glass bottle
Decorum, decency, order
Décrement, decrease, waste
Deférence, respect, submission
Delegate, a deputy
Delinquent, an offender
Demureness, affected modesty
Dénsity, thickness
Depéndent, one subordinate
Deponent, an evidence
Députy, a lieutenant
Destiny, an unalterable state
Detriment, loss, damage
Diadem, a royal crown
Diagram, a scheme
Dialect, a peculiar speech
Dialogue, a discourse
Diamond, a precious stone
Diary, a day-book
Dictátor, an absolute magistrate
Director, a guide or manager
Disaster, a misfortune
Discipline, good order
Dishónour, disgrace
Disputant, a disputer
Dissénter, a nonconformist
Disturbance, disorder, trouble
Dividend, a part, a share
Divisor, a number that divides
Dócument, an instruction
Drapery, the cloth trade
Duellist, one who fights a duel
Easiness, flexibility, rest
Ecliptic, a circle of the sphere
E'ffigy, an image, a likeness
Ejéctment, a writ to dispossess
Elector, one who chooses
E'legy, a funeral song
Elements, earth, water, fire, air
Elephant, a large beast
Ellípsis, an oval figure
E'logy, praise, panegyric
Embárgo, a stop put to trade
E'mbassy, a commission
Embryo, the imperfect state of any thing
Eminence, height
Emperor, a sovereign prince
Emphasis, the strength of pronunciation
Empiric, a quack
Endórsement, a superscription
Endowment, a natural gift
E'nergy, force, efficacy
Enginéer, an artist
Enígma, a riddle
E'nmity, hatred, malice
Ensámple, an example
E'nterprise, an attempt
Enticement, an allurement
E'ntity, a being
Epicure, one wholly given to luxury
Epigram, a short witty poem
Epilogue, a speech at the end of a play
Epistle, a letter

E'pitaph, an inscription
Equátor, the equinoctial line
E'quipage, attendance
Equity, justice
Eríngo, the sea-holly
E'stimate, calculation, value
Evidence, testimony, proof
Exácter, an extortioner
Examine, disquisition, enquiry
Example, a precedent
E'xcellence, dignity, rank
Excéptor, an objector
E'xcrement, human dung
Exercise, employment, use
Exhórter, one who exhorts
Exilement, banishment
Existence, a state of being
Ex'orcist, a conjuror [siasm
Ecstasy, excessive joy, enthu-
Faculty, ability, talent
Falconer, a trainer of hawks
Fallacy, a fallacious argument
Falsity, a lie, a cheat
Fanátic, an enthusiast
Fárrier, a shoer of horses
Favourite, a darling
Fellowship, a partnership
Festivál, a feast or holiday
Filament, a slender thread
Finery, fine attire
Firmament, the sky
Fishery, the trade of fishing
Fistula, an ulcer
Flagelet, a small flute
Flattery, false praise
Foppishness, ostentation
Forester, a keeper of a forest
Forfeiture, a fine, a penalty
Forgery, a counterfeit
Fortitude, courage, bravery
Frowárdness, peevishness
Fruitfulness, fertility
Fulfilment, accomplishment
Fúneral, a burial
Furniture, goods, utensils
Fustiness, mouldiness
Gainfulness, lucrativeness
Gainlessness, unprofitableness
Gainsáyer, an opponent
Gállantry, intrigue, bravery
Gallery, a sort of balcony
Gardener, one who cultivates a
Garniture, ornament [garden
General, a military officer
Genius, nature, fancy
Gibberish, nonsensical talk
Glazier, a worker in glass
Glimmering, a faint light
Government, rule, dominion
Governor, a ruler
Granary, a storehouse for corn
Grazier, one who feeds cattle
Gravity, sobriety, weight
Guardian, a trustee [lery
Gunnery, the science of artil-
Habitude, custom, familiarity
Harbinger, a forerunner
Harmony, agreement [ment
Harpsichord, a musical instru-
Hemisphere, half of the globe
Herbalist, one skilled in plants
Hermitage, a hermit's cell
Heroism, quality of a hero
Hexagon, a figure of six sides
History, a narration of events
Honesty, justice, truth
Hospital, a house for the sick
Humourist, a whimsical person
Hurricane, a violent storm
Hyacinth, a flower so called
Hyéna, a fierce animal
Hy'pocrite, a dissembler
Idiom, a mode of speaking
Idiot, a fool, a natural [ledg
Ignorance, a want of know
Impéachment, an accusation
I'mplement, a tool, a utensil
Impóstor, a deceiver, a cheat
I'ncident, a casualty
Incisure, a cut, a wound

Incitement, a motive
Inclosure, a space inclosed
I'ncrement, an increase
Indénture, a deed, a covenant
I'ndigo, a plant used for dying
Indúcement, a motive
Indulgence, fondness
I'ndustry, diligence
Infancy, childhood
Infantry, foot soldiers
Inference, a conclusion drawn from previous arguments
Influence, an ascendant power
Infringement, violation
I'njury, mischief, hurt
Innocence, purity, chastity
Inqúiry, a search
I'nstrument, a tool, a deed of contract
Insúrance, a security from fire
I'ntercourse, correspondence
Interest, influence, advantage
Interim, the mean time
Interlude, a farce
Intérment, a burial
Interstice, a space between two things
I'nterval, a vacant space
Interview, a mutual conference
Intru'der, an interloper
Inventer, a contriver
I'rony, keen satire
Javelin, a kind of spear
Jealousy, suspicion in love
Jeweller, a dealer in jewels
Jubilee, a year of festivity
Judaism, the Jewish religion
Kidnapper, a man-seller
Kilderkin, a small barrel
Knavery, deceitful dealing
Labyrinth, a maze
Laity, the common people
Larceny, a petty theft
Latinist, one skilled in Latin
Latitude, breadth, width
Lavender, an herb
Lechery, lasciviousness

Legacy, a bequest
Legátion, an embassy
Lénity, mildness, tenderness
Leprosy, an inveterate scurvy
Lethargy, drowsiness
Levity, vanity, lightness
Libertine, a dissolute liver
Liberty, freedom
Lieuténant, an officer, deputy
Ligament, a band, a thread
Liturgy, a form of prayer
Logarithms, artificial numbers
Longitude, distance from east to west
Lottery, a game of chance
Loyalty, fidelity to a prince
Luxury, voluptuousness
Madrigal, a pastoral song
Magazine, a storehouse
Mágistrate, a justice of peace
Magnitude, greatness
Mahomet, the Turkish impostor
Maintenance, sustenance
Malady, a distemper, disease
Manager, a conductor
Mandámus, a writ
Manœuvre, skilful management
Máriner, a seaman
Marmalade, a sweetmeat
Martyrdom, death of a martyr
Masquerade, masked assembly
Mássacre, carnage, slaughter
Medicine, a physical remedy
Medium, a middle state
Mellowness, maturity
Melody, music, harmony
Memory, rememberance
Mendicant, a beggar
Menstruum, a dissolvent fluid
Merchandise, goods, trade
Merriment, mirth, jollity
Messenger, one sent on errands
Metaphor, a figure in rhetoric
Meteor, a vapour
Microscope, a magnifying glass

Milliner, a seller of ribands
Minister, a preacher
Miracle, a wonder
Miscreant, a vile wretch
Misery, calamity
Misfórtune, ill luck
Mittimus, a warrant
Mockery, derision, sport
Modesty, bashfulness
Modeller, a contriver
Modicum, a small portion
Moiety, one half
Monarchy, kingly government
Monastery, a convent
Monitor, an adviser
Monument, a tomb, a statue
Moralist, one skilled in morals
Mountainéer, a highlander
Móuntebank, a quack
Moveables, goods, chattels
Muculent, viscous, slimy
Multitude, a number of people
Mummery, buffoonery
Murderer, one who kills another
Muséum, a study or library
Musketóon, a blunderbuss
Mu'tiny, sedition, a revolt
Myriad, the number 10,000
Mystery, a secret, a trade
Narrative, a relation, a story
Narrátor, an historian
Nátural, an idiot, a fool
Nicety, minute exactness
Novelty, newness
Nudity, nakedness
Nunnery, residence for nuns
Nutriment, nourishment
Obe'isance, an act of reverence
O'belisk, a magnificent pillar
Octagon, a figure of eight equal sides
Oculist, one who professes to cure distempers of the eyes
Offénder, a criminal
O'ffering, a sacrifice
Officer, a commander in an army
Oppónent, a rival
O'rator, an eloquent person
Ordinance, a holy rite
Organist, a player on an organ
Orison, a prayer, a supplication
Orifice, a perforation
Origin, source, derivation
Ornament, decoration
Overture, a proposal
Palisa'des, small light pales
Pa'nnier, a wicker basket
Parable, a similitude
Paradise, a place of bliss
Paradox, a puzzling assertion
Paragraph, part of a discourse
Paramour, a lover
Parasite, a flatterer, a fawner
Parentage, birth, kindred
Parity, equality, likeness
Parta'ker, a sharer
Pa'rticle, a small part of matter
Partisa'n, the leader of a party
Pa'rvity, littleness
Pasturage, pasture
Patriarch, a chief bishop
Patriot, a public benefactor
Patronage, protection
Paucity, fewness, brevity
Peasantry, the country people
Pedagogue, a pedant
Pedestal, the base of a pillar
Pedigree, family or descent
Pelican, a bird

Period, a full stop or end
Perjury, false swearing
Perquisite, extraordinary profit
Personage, a person of rank
Perúsal, a reading over
Péstilence, the plague
Pigeon, a bird well known
Pinion, a wing or feather
Pinnacle, the highest top
Pleurisy, a disease
Poetry, metrical composition
Policy, craft, prudence
Polity, civil government
Polygon, a figure of many angles
Pomegranate, a fruit
Popery, the Popish religion
Populace, the common people
Porphyry, a fine marble
Portraiture, picture from life
Potentate, a sovereign prince
Poulterer, one who sells fowls
Preámble, an introduction
Précedent, an example
Precéptor, a master or tutor
Précipice, a steep place
Preference, a preferring
Prejudice, damage, injury
Premium, a reward
Presbyter, a priest, an elder
Prescience, foreknowledge
President, a ruler
Principle, a fundamental truth
Privilege, a peculiar advantage
Privity, knowledge, consent
Probity, honesty
Procédure, progress
Pródigy, a surprising thing
Progeny, offspring
Prophecy, a prediction
Propósal, an offer
Próselyte, a convert
Prostitute, a hireling
Providence, foresight
Próviso, a stipulation
Psálmody, a singing of psalms
Punishment, chastisement
Purity, innocence
Puritan, a demure person
Purvéyor, a provider
Pyr'amid, a tapering figure
Quadrangle, a figure of four angles
Quadrature, squareness
Quality, condition, nature
Quandáry, doubt, difficulty
Quántity, bigness, extent
Quarantine, a separation
Rampire, a bank of earth
Rarity, a fine or scarce thing
Ratio, proportion, relation
Ravishment, rapture, a rape
Recital, a rehearsal
Réctangle, a right angle
Rectitude, uprightness
Rectory, a church living
Reference, act of referring
Regency, deputed government
Regicide, a king killer
Regimen, rule of diet
Register, a book of records
Rehéarsal, a previous recital
Reluctance, unwillingness
Re'medy, a cure, reparation
Remittance, return of money
Rencounter, a sudden combat
Rendezvóus, a place of meeting
Re'negade, an apostate
Repartee', a witty reply
Repe'ntance, penitence
Reprisal, a seizure
Republic, a commonwealth
Requital, a reward
Resemblance, a likeness
Resentment, a sense of injury
Re'sidence, a place of abode
Residue, the remainder
Resistance, opposition
Respondent, one who answers
Re'tinue, attendants
Retirement, privacy

Retrenchment, reduction
Re'venue, yearly profit
Revi'sal, a second examination
Rha'psody, a confused writing
Rhetoric, the art of speaking
Rheumatism, an acute disease
Ribaldry, mean discourse
Ritual, a book of rites
Royalty, kingship
Rudiments, first principles
Ruffian, a desperate villain
Runagate, a fugitive
Sacrament, a holy sign
Sacrilege, church robbery
Salary, a stated hire
Saltpe'tre, a mineral salt
Sa'nctity, holiness, purity
Sanity, health, soundness
Sapience, prudence, wisdom
Saturday, the seventh day
Satirist, a writer of satire
Scavenger, a gatherer of dirt
Scrivener, a writer
Scrutiny, search, enquiry
Secresy, retirement
Sectary, one of any sect
Section, a division
Sentiment, opinion, thought
Sepulchre, a grave or tomb
Serena'de, nocturnal music
Se'ries, order, continuance
Servitor, a waiter at a college
Servitude, bondage
Settlement, a settled income
Signature, a sign or mark
Sillabub, milk and wine
Simony, the buying and selling of church livings
Skeleton, animal bones entire
Solitude, retirement
Sonnete'er, a trifling poet
Sŏphister, a cavilling disputer
Sorcery, magic, witchcraft
Sovereign, a king a prince
Species, a kind or sort
Specimen, a sample
Spectátor, a looker on
Spéctacle, a public sight
Speculum, a looking-glass
Strangury, a disease
Strappádo, a chastisement
Strátagem, an artifice
Suavity, pleasantness
Subsidy, an aid, a grant
Subterfuge, evasion, shift
Suicide, self-murder
Sullenness, stubbornness
Summary, an abridgement
Supplement, an addition
Surgery, practice of a surgeon
Surrogate, a deputy
Survéyor, a measurer of land
Survivor, the longest liver
Sy'cophant, a flatterer
Symmetry, proportion
Symphony, harmony of sounds
Synagogue, a place of worship
Synópsis, a brief view
Táffety, a sort of foreign silk
Tapestry, figured hangings
Telescope, a glass for viewing distant objects
Temperance, moderation
Tendency, drift, course
Tenement, a dwelling-house
Terrier, a dog
Testament, a will
Testátor, one who gives by will
Théatre, a play-house
Tobácco, an Indian plant
Trágedy, a mournful play
Treasury, a place for money
Triangle, a figure of three sides
Tribúnal, a judgement-seat
Trinity, the Godhead
Turmeric, a root for dying
Turpentine, a sort of oil
Turpitude, vileness
Tympany, a hard swelling
Tyra'nny, cruel government

Umbrélla, a screen from rain
U'nity, union, concord
Universe, the whole world
Urinal, a glass for urine
Usurer, one who lends for gain
Uténsil, an instrument or tool
U'tterance, power of speech
Vacancy, a vacant place
Vacuum, an empty space
Vagabond, an idle fellow
Vanity, petty pride
Variance, difference
Vassalage, subjection
Vatican, a library at Rome
Vehicle, a carriage
Venery, lustfulness
Venison, the flesh of deer
Ventricle, the stomach
Venturer, one who hazards
Verdigris, the rust of brass
Verity, truth
Vertigo, a giddiness
Vicarage, benefice of a vicar
Vigilánce, watchfulness
Villager, inhabitant of a village
Vintager, a manager of grapes
Violet, a flower
Virágo, a turbulent woman
Volcano, a burning mountain
Vótary, a person devoted
Votaress, a female votary
Wagoner, a wagon driver
Wantonness, lasciviousness
Warrener, keeper of a warren
Weariness, fatigue
Wednesday, the fourth day
Whitsunday, the seventh Sunday after Easter
Widower, one who has lost his wife
Wilderness, a wild place
Wretchedness, misery
Yeomanry, a body of yeomen
Yesterday, the day last past
Zodiac, a circle in the heavens
Zoology, the science of animals

TABLE V.

NOUNS ADJECTIVE, OF THREE SYLLABLES, ACCENTED AND EXPLAINED.

Abortive, untimely
A'bsolute, unlimited
Abstérgent, cleansing
A'bstinent, abstemious
Abusive, insolent
Abundant, plentiful
Accordant, agreeing
A'ccurate, exact, correct
Affable, courteous
Affrontive, abusive
Alamode, fashionable
A'liquant, uneven
Altérnate, successive
A'mbient, encompassing
Amorous, apt to fall in love
Ancient, old
Annual, yearly
Anxious, much concerned [plain
Appárent, manifest,
Applauding, commending
A'pposite, fit
Aqueous, waterish
Arrogant, proud, assuming
Astringent, binding
Attentive, heedful
Authentic, of good authority
Autumnal, belonging to autumn
Bárbarous, cruel
Benúmbed, deprived of feeling
Besieged, encompassed
Béstial, beastly
Boisterous, unruly, stormy
Capital, great, chief
Casual, by chance
Catholic, universal, general
Circular, round
Circumspect, watchful, wise [pertinent
Clamorous, noisy, im-
Coéqual, equal to another [fied
Cómpetent, fit, quali-
Conical, pleasant, witty [civil
Complaisánt, obliging,
Concéited, proud, affected
Conclusive, ending, decisive

Conducive, profitable, helpful [proper
Cóngruous, convenient,
Conjugal, matrimonial
Consistent, agreeable to
Cóntinent, chaste
Contingent, accidental, casual
Cónversant, familiar
Copious, full, abounding
Corporal, bodily, gross
Corrósive, fretting, gnawing [credit
Crédible, worthy of
Credulous, apt to believe [ment
Critical, of nice judge-
Cubical, belonging to a cube
Culpable, blameworthy
Cumbersome, troublesome
Cursory, hasty, short
Debonáir, courteous, sprightly [ten
Décimal, belonging to
Decisive, conclusive
Defective, wanting, imperfect
Definite, limited
Delicate, dainty, neat
Depéndent, subject to
Désolate, uninhabited
Desperate, furious, dangerous
Despónding, despairing
Despotic, arbitrary
Déstitute, forsaken
Dexterous, cunning, skilful
Diffident, bashful
Diffúsive, spreading
Discordant, disagreeing
Dissolute, loose, wanton
Dissonant, untunable, jarring
Dissúasive, apt to dissuade
Diurnal, daily
Dócible, tractable
Dogmátic, positive
Dólorous, sorrowful
Doméstic, belonging to home [dropsy
Drópsical, subject to
Dubious, doubtful
Duplicate, double
Durable, lasting [east
Easterly, towards the
Eccéntric, irregular
E'dible, eatable
Efféctive, powerful
Emergent, sudden, accidental [nowned
E'minent, high, re-
Enórmous, out of rule, heinous
Erratic, wandering
Eternal, of infinite duration [ceitful
Evasive, crafty, de-
E'vident, plain, notorious
Exálted, lifted up
E'xcellent, choice, valuable
Excéssive, beyond due bounds
Exempted, privileged
Exotic, outlandish
Expensive, chargeable, costly [ous
Explicit, clear, obvi-
E'xquisite, exact, perfect
Exténsive, wide, large
External, outward
Extrinsic, on the outside
Fábulous, feigned
Factious, seditious
Fállible, that may err
Fantástic, whimsical
Féasible, practicable
Feculent, foul, muddy
Federal, belonging to covenant
Feminine, of the female kind [a fever
Feverish, tending to
Filial, belonging to a son [pish
Finical, affected, fop-
Flatulent, windy
Flexible, easy to bend, pliant
Forcible, strong, powerful [cessful
Fortunate, lucky, suc-
Frangible, brittle
Fratérnal, brotherly
Fraúdulent, crafty, deceitful
Frivolous, of no account, silly [mirth
Frolicsome, full of
Fulminant, thundering
Furious, mad, fierce
Garrulous, full of talk
Generous, liberal, bountiful
Genial, joyful, natural
Genuine, original
Gigántic, like a giant
Glóbular, round as a globe
Glorious, full of glory
Glutinous, clammy
Gluttonous, greedy, devouring
Gracious, graceful, kind
Gradual, by degrees
Hallowed, made holy
Hazardous, dangerous
Heróic, valiant
Hideous, frightful
Horrible, ghastly
Humorous, jocular
Hydrópic, dropsical
Ignoble, base
Illégal, contrary to law
Immatúre, not perfect
Immérged, plunged into
I'mminent, impending
Immódest, wanton, rude
Immoral, profane
Immortal, everlasting
Impendent, hanging over
Imperfect, unfinished
I'mpious, ungodly
Implicit, tacitly understood
Important, of great concern
Improper, inconvenient, unfit
Imprudent, unwise

I'mpudent, shameless
Ince'ntive, stirring up
Incessant, without ceasing
Inclusive, comprehending
Incomple'te, imperfect
Incompact, not close fastened
Incónstant, uncertain
Incorre'ct, faulty, erroneous
Incorrupt, untainted
Increate, not created
Inde'cent, unbecoming
Indented, notched
I'ndigent, needy, poor
Indire'ct, unfair, unhandsome
Indiscreet, imprudent
I'ndolent, lazy, careless
Infamous, scandalous
Infe'rnal, hellish
Infertile, barren, unfruitful
I'nfinite, without end
Infúsed, soaked or steeped
Inherent, innate
Inhuman, barbarous
I'nnocent, not guilty
Insecúre, not safe
Insipid, tasteless, flat
I'nsolent, saucy, proud
Inte'rnal, inward
Intestate. dying without a will
I'ntimate, familiar
Intre'pid, fearless, undaunted
Intrinsic, inward, real
Invalid, not good in law
Invective, railing, reproachful
Jócular, pleasant, merry
Jovial, gay, cheerful
Juvenile, youthful
Lacónic, brief, concise
Lácteal, milky
Lateral, sideways
Laudable, commendable
Laxative, loosening
Legible, easy to be read
Lenitive, assuaging, healing
Limited, bounded
Lineal, belonging to a line
Literal, according to the letter
Logical, belonging to logic
Lubricous, slippery, uncertain
Lucrative, gainful
Luminous, full of light
Lunatic, distracted
Luscious, over sweet
Maje'stic, noble, stately
Malignant, hurtful
Mánifest, clear, evident
Marginal, placed in the margin
Maritime, belonging to the sea
Martial, warlike, valiant
Masculine, manly
Mate'rnal, motherly
Me'nial, domestic
Menstrual, monthly
Me'talline, of the nature of metal
Militant, fighting
Mimical, apish
Mineral, belonging to mines
Moderate, temperate, sober
Meméntous, important
Morbific, causing diseases
Móveable, what may be moved
Mountainous, hilly, irregular
Multiform, of many shapes
Musical, belonging to music
Mutable, subject to change
Mutinous, seditious
Mutual, alike on both sides
Mystical, belonging to mystery
Natural, easy, free, unaffected
Nauseous, loathsome
Nebulous, cloudy
Negative, denying
Negligent, careless
Neighbourly, friendly
Niggardly, sordid, mean
Noctúrnal, nightly
Nóxious, hurtful
Numeral, belonging to number
Numerous, great in number
Nutritive, nourishing
Obdurate, hardened, obstinate
Obliging, civil, courteous
O'bstinate, stubborn
Obsolete, out of date
Obvious, clear, plain
Ocular, belonging to the eyes
Odious, hateful
Odorous, sweet smelling
Offe'nsive, displeasing
O'minous, ill-boding
Operóse, laborious
Opportune, convenient
O'pposite, over against
Opulent, wealthy
Orderly, regular
Orthodox, sound in faith
Overplus, over and above
Paci'fic, peaceable
Pa'lpable, manifest, clear
Pare'ntal, belonging to parents
Pa'rallel, equal to
Partial, biased
Passable, that may be passed
Pastoral, rural
Pate'rnal, fatherly
Pathetic, moving the passions
Pa'thos, warmth, feeling
Pectoral, belonging to the breast
Pellúcid, clear, bright
Pe'nitent, sorrowful, repentant
Perilous, dangerous
Permanent, lasting
Perple'xed, confounded
Pe'rsonal, belonging to a person

Persua'sive, apt to persuade [purpose
Pe'rtinent, fit for the
Pervious, easy to be passed [ish
Petulent, saucy, peev-
Physical, belonging to physic
Piteous, sad, grievous
Plausible, seemingly fair
Plenary, full, complete
Plenteous, copious
Popular, beloved by the people [carried
Portable, that may be
Positive, dogmatical
Possible, that may be done [death
Posthumous, after
Potable, drinkable
Practical, belonging to practice [saucy
Pragmátic, over busy,
Precedent, foregoing
Preceptive, belonging to precept
Prévalent, predominant
Previous, antecedent
Primary, principal
Primitive, ancient
Probable, likely
Prodigal, lavish, vain-glorious
Projécted, contrived
Prolific, apt to breed, fruitful
Próminent, jutting out
Prosperous, fortunate
Puerile, childish
Puissant, powerful
Púnctual, nice, exact
Quadrátic, four square
Quádruped, a fourfooted animal
Quadruple, four-fold
Quarrelsome, apt to quarrel [plain
Querulous, apt to com-
Quie'scent, at rest
Quintuple, five-fold
Radiant, bright, shining [the root
Radical, belonging to
Recu'mbent, in a lying posture
Redundant, abounding
Refracted, broken again
Refulgent, shining, bright [rule
Re'gular, according to
Relative, having relation to
Renewed, began afresh
Renowned, famous
Réprobate, vile
Repúgnant, contrary to
Réquisite, necessary
Resolute, bold
Resple'ndent, shining
Re'trograde, going backward
Reverend, worthy of veneration
Reve'rsed, turned upside down [just
Righteous, upright,
Riotous, disorderly
Romántic, idle, fabulous
Sabbatic, belonging to the sabbath
Sa'native, healing
Saturnine, melancholy, grave [well
Savoury, that relishes
Scandalous, disgraceful
Scenical, theatrical
Scorbútic, having the scurvy [cise
Scrúpulous, nice, pre-
Scurrilous, scandalous
Secular, temporal, worldly
Seizable, that may be seized
Sensible, perceptible, witty [sense
Sensitive, that has
Sensual, given to pleasure
Serious, sober, grave
Serpentine, winding
Singular, particular
Specious, fair in appearance
Sperma'tic, full of seed
Sphe'rical, round
Splene'tic, full of spleen
Spu'rious, counterfeit, false [orous
Strenuous, active, vig
Submissive, humble
Successful, fortunate
Successive, which follows
Súmptuous, rich, costly
Superfi'ne, very fine
Suspe'nded, put off
Te'mporal, belonging to time [held
Tenable, that may be
Tenébrious, full of darkness
Te'rrible, dreadful
Timorous, fearful
Titular, that bears a title
Towardly, obedient
Tractable, easily managed [tor
Traitorous, like a trai-
Transcéndent, excellent
Tránsient, passing away
Transpa'rent, bright, clear
Tre'acherous, perfidious
Treme'ndous, dreadful
Tripartite, divided in three parts
Triplicate, triple, or three-fold
Trivial, of small concern
Turbulent, boisterous, disturbing
Typical, belonging to a figure [rant
Tyrannous, like a ty-
Ulcerous, full of sores
Ultimate, final, utmost
Une'qual, not equal
U'niform, regular, even
Unwieldy, heavy, inactive
U'rinous, belonging to urine
Valiant, stout, brave
Various, different
Vehement, earnest
Vendible, saleable
Venomous, poisonous
Venial, pardonable

Venturesome, bold, hardy
Vertical, overhead
Vicious, wicked, lewd
Vigorous, lively, strong
Villanous, base, wicked
Vincible, that may be overcome
Vindictive, revengeful
Violent, boisterous, high
Viperous, of the viper kind
Virtuous, endowed with virtue
Virulent, of venomous quality
Visible, that may be seen
Visual, belonging to the sight
Volatile, airy, light
Voluble, quick of speech
Whimsical, full of fancies
Withered, dried, faded
Wonderful, surprising

TABLE VI.

VERBS OF THREE SYLLABLES, ACCENTED AND EXPLAINED.

Abándon, to forsake
A'bdicate, to renounce
Abólish, to destroy
A'brogate, to make void
Acquiésce, to comply with
A'ctuate, to move, to quicken
Aggrandise, to make great
Agitate, to put in motion
Antedate, to date before time
Appertáin, to belong to
A'rbitrate, to determine
Ascertáin, to establish, to assure
Cálculate, to reckon up
Celebrate, to make famous
Certify, to assure
Circumscribe, to limit
Circumvent, to deceive
Civilize, to make courteous
Clarify, to make clear
Compénsate, to make amends
Comprehénd, to contain
Condescend, to comply with
Cónsecrate, to dedicate
Constitute, to appoint
Consúmate, to perfect
Contemplate, to meditate
Continue, to abide, to last
Contribute, to give something
Cóntrovert, to dispute
Correspónd, to write to one another
Coúnterfeit, to imitate
Decipher, to unravel
Décorate, to adorn
Demérit, to deserve ill
Demolish, to destroy
Demonstrate, to show plainly
Deposit, to trust with another
Déprecate, to pray against
Derogate, to detract from
Dignify, to advance, to honour
Disabúse, to undeceive
Disagree, to differ
Disallow, not to allow
Disannul, to make void
Disapprove, to blame
Discompose, to trouble
Disembark, to go on shore
Disengage, to get off
Disesteem, not to esteem
Dishónour, to disgrace
Dislocate, to put out of joint
Disoblige, to displease
Dispárage, to speak ill of
Dispirit, to discourage
Disposséss, to deprive
Disqúiet, to trouble
Disregárd, to slight
Disrélish, to dislike
Dissipate, to disperse or scatter
Distinguish, to discern between
Distribute, to divide or share
Disunite, to separate
Dógmatize, to assert positively
Educate, to nourish, to instruct
Elevate, to lift up
Embárrass, to clog, to hinder

Embellish, to beautify
Enamel, to vary with spots
Encircle, to encompass
Encounter, to fight with
Encumber, to overload
Enervate, to weaken
Enfeeble, to make weak
Engender, to beget, to breed
Enliven, to make brisk or lively
Entangle, to ensnare
Entertáin, to receive kindly
Envé'nom, to infect with poison
Environ, to enclose
Establish, to settle
Execute, to perform
Exhi'bit, to produce, to show
E'xpedite, to hasten
Expiate, to atone for
Explicate, to unfold, to explain
Exti'nguish, to put out
Extricate, to disentangle
Exu'ndate, to overflow
Fa'lsify, to counterfeit
Fascinate, to bewitch
Fluctuate, to waver in opinion
Fortify, to fence, to make strong
Generate, to beget
Gratify, to requite
Hesitate, to doubt
Idolize, to worship, to adore
Illu'strate, to explain
Imagine, to fancy
I'mitate, to do the like
Importu'ne, to request
Impre'gnate, to make fruitful
Imprison, to put in prison
Incarnate, to clothe with flesh
Incommo'de, to annoy
Incu'lcate, to advise often
Incumber, to clog, to hinder
Incurvate, to bow or bend
Indicate, to declare, to show
Indispo'se, to make unfit
Inge'nder, to beget, to produce
Inhabit, to dwell in
I'nnovate, to introduce novelties
Instigate, to set on, to provoke
Institute, to appoint, to ordain
Interce'de, to entreat for
Intercept, to obstruct
Interfere, to intermeddle
Interject, to cast between
Intermix, to mix with
Interpose, to intermeddle
Inte'rpret, to explain
Interru'pt, to hinder, to stop
Intersect, to cut in two
Intersperse, to scatter between
Intervene, to come between
In'timate, to point out indirectly
Inti'tle, to give right to
Introdu'ce, to bring in
Inve'igle, to allure, to entice
I'nvocate, to call upon
Irritate, to provoke, to stir up
Justify, to clear one's self
Lacerate, to tear in peaces
Levigate, to reduce to powder
Macerate, to make clean
Magnify, to enlarge
Manacle, to bind, to fetter
Mediate, to intercede
Medicate, to heal, to cure
Meditate, to think upon
Mention, to take notice of
Methodize, to put in order
Misca'rry, not to succeed
Misconstrue, to interpret amiss
Mi'tigate, to pacify, to ease
Modify, to shape, to qualify
Mollify, to make soft
Mortify, to corrupt, to vex
Multiply, to increase
Nauseate, to loathe, to abhor
Nominate, to appoint
Notify, to make known
Nullify, to make void
Numerate, to count, to number
Obligate, to bind to oblige

Occupy, to possess, to use
Operate, to work
Palliate, to extenuate
Paraphrase, to explain
Penetrate, to enter into
Perforate, to pierce through
Perpetrate, to commit
Persevére, to continue stedfast
Pérsonate, to represent a person
Petrify, to turn into stone
Pinion, to pin or bind fast
Pre-exist, to exist before hand
Prohibit, to forbid
Promulgate, to make public
Próstitute, to make common
Putrify, to corrupt
Qualify, to make fit
Radicate, to take root
Rarify, to make thin
Ratify, to confirm
Re-admit, to receive again
Re-assign, to make over again
Recognize, to acknowledge
Recollect, to call to mind
Recommend, to speak well of
Récreate, to refresh
Rectify, to correct, to amend
Redoúble, to double again
Régulate, to set in order
Re-embárk, to take ship again
Re-enforce, to strengthen
Re-imburse, to repay
Re-possess, to possess again
Represent, to make appear
Réprimand, to rebuke
Ruminate, to reflect, to muse
Separate, to part or divide
Sequéster, to put aside
Signalize, to distinguish
Solemnize, to celebrate
Specify, to mention expressly
Speculate, to consider, to hazard
Stigmatize, to disgrace
Stipulate, to covenant
Stupify, to make dull
Substitute, to put in another's place
Suffocate, to stifle or choke
Superádd, to add over and above
Superscribe, to write over
Supersede, to suspend
Supervise, to oversee
Surrénder, to yield up
Sym'pathize, to suffer with
Tantalize, to mock, to balk
Terminate, to limit, to bound
Tolerate, to suffer, to bear with
Transfi'gure, to change in shape
Undermíne, to injure secretly
Vérify, to prove, to make good
Versify, to make verses
Vilify, to debase
Vindicate, to defend, to justify
Violate, to break, to transgress
Vitiate, to corrupt, to deprave

TABLE VII.

NOUNS SUBSTANTIVE OF FOUR SYLLABLES, ACCENTED AND EXPLAINED.

Abintéstate, an heir to one dying without a will
Abólishment, a destroying
Abortion, miscarriage
A'ccessary, a helper or adviser
Accómplishment, a fulfilling
A'ccurateness, exactness
Acidity, sharpness
Acknowledgement, confession
A'crimony, tartness
Addition, an adding
Admíssion, entrance upon
Adoléscence, youthfulness
Adóption, free choice
Adversity, affliction
Advertency, carefulness

Advertisement, intelligence
Affidávit, witness upon oath
Affínity, relation
Alabáster, a sort of soft marble
Alácrity, cheerfulness
Allegiance, obedience
A'llegory, a figure in rhetoric
Allúsion, a hint, an implication
Ambition, an earnest desire
Analysis, a separation of the parts
Anathema, a solemn curse
Anatomy, dissection
Annuity, a yearly rent
Antagonist, an adversary
Antipathy, natural aversion
Antiquity, oldness
Anxiety, trouble of mind
Apology, an excuse
Apostacy, a falling away from
Apostrophe, a turning of the course of speech, a mark of contraction (')
Architécture, art of building
Arithmetic, science of numbers
Artillery, great guns
Ascension, the act of rising
Asperity, roughness
Aspersion, a slander [stars
Astrology, prediction from the
Astronomy, knowledge of the heavenly bodies [hearers
Aúditory, an assembly of
Authórity, rule or power
Barbarians, barbarous people
Barometer, a weather-glass
Battalion, a large body of men
Benefáctor, one bestowing ben-
Benéficence, kindness [efit
Benevolence, good-will
Benignity, goodness
Bisection, the cutting in two
Bréviary, a mass book
Británnia, Great Britain
Brutality, beastliness
Búrgomaster, a magistrate
Calámity, misfortune
Calidity, heat
Captivity, slavery
Carnality, fleshliness
Carnation, a flower
Cásualty, chance
Celérity, swiftness
Célibacy, single life [men
Centúrion, an officer over 100
Céremony, a formal civility
Certificate, a written testimony
Cessation, a ceasing
Chronology, history of time
Circumference, a circle [tion
Citation, a summons, a quota-
Civility, courtesy
Coaction, compulsion
Coadjútor, a fellow-helper
Coalescence, concretion
Cognítion, knowledge, trial
Coherency, agreement
Cohesion, a sticking together
Collation, an entertainment
Collection, a gathering
Collegiate, a fellow student
Collision, a striking together
Collusion, deceit
Combustion, a burning
Comedian, a stage player
Cómmentary, an interpretation
Commissary, a church officer
Commission, a trust
Commodity, goods
Cómmonalty, common people
Commótion, a disturbance
Community, a society
Compendium, an abridgment
Cómpetency, sufficiency
Complácency, civility
Complexion, colour of the face
Completion, a fulfilling [ther
Compression, a pressing toge-
Compulsion, constraint
Compunction, remorse

Concavity, inside hollowness
Conception, a notion
Concession, grant, permission
Concinnity, aptness
Conclusion, the end
Concoction, digestion
Condensity, thickness
Conformity, compliance
Congruity, consistency
Conjunction, union with
Connexion, relation to
Consectary, an inference
Conservator, a keeper
Contagion, infection
Contention, strife
Contingency, an accident
Contraction, a shortning
Contrition, real repentance
Cóntumacy, stubbornness
Contumely, reproach
Contúsion, a bruise
Convention, an assembly
Convexity, outside roundness
Córollary, deduction, surplus
Corpulency, grossness of body
Corrósion, a gnawing
Corruption, rottenness
Credentials, letters of credit
Credulity, readiness to believe
Damnation, condemnation
Debauchery, lewdness
Deception, a deceiving
Decision, a determining
Declension, a decaying
Declivity, steepness
Decoction, a seething
Decursion, a running down
Deduction, a taking from
Defluxion, a flowing down
Deformity, ugliness
Dejection, a casting down
De'licacy, niceness, softness
Demócracy, government by the people
Demoniac, one possessed by [the devil
Depression, a pressing down
Derision, a mocking
Descension, a descending
Desertion, a forsaking
Desperádo, a desperate fellow
Despo'ndency, a despairing
Detrusion, a thrusting down
Dexterity, readiness, skill
Diagonal, a slant line
Digestion, concoction
Dimension, bulk, capacity
Directory, that which directs
Disagree'ment, discord
Disco'mfiture, overthrow
Discretion, wisdom
Discussion, an examination
Disjunction, a disjoining
Disloyalty, want of allegiance
Dismission, a sending away
Dispansion, a spreading abroad
Disparity, unlikeness
Dispersion, a spreading
Dissension, strife
Dissuasion, persuading against
Disunion, division
Diversity, variety
Docility, teachableness
Donation, a grant
Doxology, a divine hymn
Duration, continuance
Ebriety, drunkenness
Edition, impression of a book
E'fficacy, force, strength
Effigy, image, likeness
Effúsion, a pouring out
Emergency, casualty
E'minency, excellency
Emissary, a spy
Emótion, a moving
Empyreum, the highest heaven
Enco'mium, commendation
Enormity, heinousness
Enthusiast, one who fancies himself inspired
E'picurism, gluttony

Epiphany, a manifestation
Epitome, a short account
Equality, sameness
Equation, a making equal
Erection, a raising upright
Eruption, a breaking out
Escutcheon, a coat of arms
Evasion, a shift or escape
Eviction, a convincing
Exaction, an unjust demand
E'xcellency, a title of honour
Exclúsion, a shutting out
Excursion, a ramble
Executor, one who executes a person's will
Exemption, a privilege
E'xigency, need
Expánsion, a spreading abroad
Extension, a stretching out
Extinction, a putting out
Extortion, unlawful game
Extraction, a drawing out
Extrusion, a driving out
Facility, easiness
Fe'bruary, the second month
Fecúndity, fruitfulness
Ferocity, fierceness
Fertility, plentifulness
Fidelity, faithfulness
Fixation, a fixing
Flátulency, windiness
Fluidity, a flowing
Formality, ceremony
Formation, a fashioning
Foundation, the lowest part
Fragility, brittleness
Fraternity, brotherhood
Fraúdulency, deceitfulness
Frigidity, coldness, impotency
Frugality, thriftiness
Fruition, enjoyment
Frustration, disappointment
Fumidity, smokiness
Futurity, the time to come
Garrulity, talkativeness
Gelidity, coldness
Gentility, good breeding
Geography, a description of the earth
Geometry, the science of measuring lines and figures
Gibbosity, a bunching out
Gilliflower, a July flower
Gladiator, a fencer
Gradátion, going step by step
Grammarian, a teacher of grammar
Gratuity, a reward
Háberdasher, a seller of small wares
Habiliment, clothing
Hilarity, cheerfulness
Hostility, open war
Humanity, courtesy
Humidity, moisture
Hyperbole, an exaggeration
Hypocrisy, deceit
Hypothesis, a supposition
Ichnography, the ground-plot
Identity, sameness
I'diotism, simplicity
Idólatry, idol worship
I'gnominy, dishonour, shame
Illátion, an inference
Illusion, sham or cheat
Immensity, boundlessness
Immodesty, wantonness
Immunity, freedom
Imparity, inequality
Impediment, hinderance
Impiety, ungodliness
I'mpotency, weakness
Impre'ssion, a stamp, influence
Improbity, dishonesty
Impunity, freedom from punishment
Inadve'rtence, heedlessness
Inánity, emptiness
Incision, a gash or cut
Incursion, an inroad of soldiers
Indignity, an affront

nduction, a leading into
naptitude, unaptness [rank
Inferiors, persons of a lower
Infinity, endlessness
Infirmary, a house for sick
Infirmity, weakness
Infusion, a pouring in
Ingratitude, unthankfulness
Injection, a casting in
Injunction, a command
Inquietude, restlessness
Inscription, a written title
Insertion, a thing inserted
Inspection, insight
Integrity, honesty
Intention, design
Intrusion, an encroachment
Inversion, a turning
Laxation, a loosening
Legality, lawfulness
Legerdemáin, slight of hand
Législator, a law-giver
Licéntiate, one having a license
Limpidity, clearness
Lineament, a feature
Literature, learning
Locálity, existence in a place
Logician, one skilled in reason-
Longevity, long life [ing
Lubricity, slipperiness
Magician, a conjuror [trate
Mágistracy, office of a magis-
Malignity, ill-nature
Maniféslo, a declaration
Mathematics, science of num-
Mátrimony, marriage [bers
Matúrity, ripeness
Máyoralty, office of a mayor
Memórial, a token
Meridian, a circle on the globe
Misdeméanor, an offence
Mónastery, a college of monks
Monition, a warning
Morality, virtue, duty
Mutation, a changing

Narration, a relation
Nativity, birth [ral causes
Náturalist, one skilled in natu
Necromancy, conjuring
Negátion, a denying
Neutrality, indifference [eye
Nictation, winking with the
Nobility, nobleness of birth
Nonentity, a thing not in being
Nonresidence, failure of resi-
Nutrition, nourishment [dence
Obdurátion, hardness of heart
Objéction, a replying against
Oblation, an offering
Obliquity, crookedness
Oblivion, forgetfulness
Obscenity, unclean speech
Obscurity, darkness, privacy
O'bstinacy, stubbornness
Obstrúction, hinderance
Optation, a desiring
Oration, a public speech
O'ratory, the art of eloquence
Original, the first beginning
Orthography, true writing
Paralogism, a false argument
Pársimony, sparingness
Partition, a division
Pátrimony, an inheritance
Patriotism, love of our country
Pavilion, a tent of state
Peninsula, land almost sur-
rounded by water
Penultima, the last syllable but
Percussion, a striking [one
Perdition, utter ruin
Perplexity, doubtfulness
Persevérance, constancy
Pervérsion, a seducing from
Petition, a request [guages
Philology, the study of lan
Philosophy, the knowledge of
natural and moral things
Phlebotomy, blood-letting
Physician, a doctor of physic

Plantation, a settlement
Plurality, more than one
Poetáster, a sorry poet
Pollútion, uncleanness
, place or situation
Precaution, forewarning
Precession, a going before
Prediction, a foretelling
Predecéssor, one going before
Pre-éminence, precedence
Prerogative, privilege
Pré sbytery, eldership
Presúmption, boldness
Pretension, claim
Prevention, hinderance
Probation, proof, trial
Procession, a solemn march
Proclivity, a tendency
Procurátor, a solicitor
Prodúction, a bringing forth
Profession, a calling or trade
Proficient, one who makes improvement
Progression, a going forward
Prolixity, tediousness
Prómontory, a rising ground
Promótion, preferment
Propensity, inclination of mind
Propinquity, nearness
Proportion, agreement
Proprietor, the proper owner
Propriety, fitness
Prosperity, success, happiness
Protection, defence
Prótestantism, the religion of protestants
Protúberance, a swelling out
Provision, food
Proximity, nearness
Pulsation, a beating of the pulse
Punctilio, a trifle
Purgation, a cleansing
Púrgatory, a place of punishment
Pyrotechny, art of fireworks
Quatérnion, the number four
Quotation, a quoting
Rapidity, swiftness
Reality, the truth of a matter
Receptacle, a storehouse
Reddition, a restoring again
Redemption, a ransoming
Reduction, a reducing
Refection, a refreshment
Reflection, meditation
Refraction, a bending
Regulátor, one who regulates
Rejéction, a casting off
Reimbúrsement, a paying back
Relátion, a kindred, a narration
Religion, the worship of God
Remission, forgiveness
Repugnancy, reluctance
Restriction, restraint
Resumption, taking again
Retention, a retaining
Retortion, a returning back
Reversion, right of inheritance
Reunion, uniting again
Rogation, an asking
Rotation, a turning round
Rotundity, roundness
Rusticity, clownishness
Sagacity, sharpness of wit
Sánctimony, holiness
Satiety, fulness
Scrutation, a searching
Seclusion, a shutting out
Sécretary, a writer
Secrétion, a separation
Security, safety
Seduction, a misleading
Sémicircle, a half circle
Seminary, a nursery
Sensátion, a perceiving by sense
Seraglio, a place for concubines
Servility, the condition of slaves
Severity, strictness
Similitude, likeness
Simplicity, honesty, foolishness
Sincerity, uprightness

Sobriety, prudent carriage
Society, company, union
Solemnity, a solemn action
Solidity, soundness, hardness
Soliloquy, a talking to one's self
Solution, an explanation
So'vereignty, supreme power
Stabi'lity, firmness, constancy
Sta'tioner, a seller of paper
Statuary, a carver of images
Stoli'dity, foolishness
Stupidity, dullness
Subjection, dependence
Sublimity, loftiness, height
Submission, obedience
Subtraction, a deduction
Subversion, ruin, destruction
Succession, a coming after
Sudation, a sweating
Suggestion, a putting in mind
Supervi'sor, an overseer
Suppréssion, putting a stop to
Supremacy, chief authority
Suspension, a cessation
Tautology, a repetition
Taxation, a laying on of taxes
Temerity, rashness
Temperature, state, disposition
Temptátion, enticement
Tenuity, smallness, thinness
Te'rritory, a compass of land
Theo'logy, divinity
Timidity, fearfulness
Tradition, a delivering down
Traduction, a propagation
Tranquillity, peace of mind
Transaction, an action done
Transcription, a writing over again
Transfusion, pouring into another
Transgression, a violation
Transition, a removal
Translation, a change, version
Tuition, the care of education
Tumidity, a swelling
Ubiquity, a being in all places
Urbanity, good breeding
Utility, profit, usefulness
Vacation, ease, leisure
Vacuity, emptiness
Validity, strength, power
Ve'getable, a plant
Velo'city, swiftness
Veracity, honesty, truth
Vermilion, a fine red colour
Ve'rsifier, a maker of verses
Vibra'tion, a shaking
Vicinity, a neighbourhood
Vicissitude, change of things
Virtuo'so, an ingenious person
Vivácity, liveliness
Vocation, a calling, employ
Volition, the act of willing

TABLE VIII.

NOUNS ADJECTIVE, OF FOUR SYLLABLES, ACCENTED AND EXPLAINED.

Abste'mious, sober, temperate
Accessible, approachable
Accide'ntal, by chance
Acco'untable, answerable for
Adorable, worthy of honor
Æthereal, heavenly, pure
Affirmative, positive
Allowable, lawful
A'lterative, changing slowly
Ambi'guous, doubtful
A'miable, lovely
Amicable, friendly
Amphi'buous, that lives upon land and water
Anonymous, without name
Antece'dent, going before

A'ntiquated, grown out of date
Applicable, that may be applied
Arbitrary, absolute, free
Arti'culate, distinct in speech
Assiduous, diligent
Audacious, bold, daring
Auricular, belonging to the ear
Auspicious, happy, prosperous
Beati'fic, blissful
Bitu'minous, clammy
Botanical, belonging to herbs
Cadaverous, relating to a dead body
Canonical, regular, scriptural
Capacious, large
Carnivorous, feeding on flesh
Chimerical, imaginary
Circumjácent, round about
Coeternal, equal in eternity
Coexistent, being together
Coi'ncident, happening together
Collateral, not direct, sideways
Combustible, apt to take fire
Commodious, convenient
Comparative, capable of comparison
Compatible, consistent
Compendious, brief, concise
Co'mplicated, folded together
Comprehe'nsive, capacious, full
Conspi'cuous, easy to be seen
Contiguous, that is near
Convivial, social
Corporeal, bodily, material
Cústomary, common
Cyli'ndrical, like a cylinder
Decennial, of ten years
Declarative, explanatory
Deducible, that may be inferred
Deficient, wanting
Definitive, decisive, positive
Delectable, delightful
Deliberate, prudent, advised
Delicious, pleasant to the taste
Delirious, light-headed
Determinate, positive
Detestable, vile, hateful
Di'latory, full of delays
Disaffe'cted, not pleased with
Disso'lvable, capable of dissolution
Distributive, which serves to distribute
Divisible, that may be divided
Dogmatical, positive
Effeminate, womanish
Egregious, singular, rare, great
Elaborate, done with exactness
Elliptical, belonging to an oval
Episcopal, belonging to a bishop
Equivalent, of equal worth
Erroneous, full of error
Essential, necessary
E'xecrable, hateful, accursed
Exo'rbitant, extravagant
Expedient, necessary
Extempore, without study
Facetious, pleasant, witty
Fallacious, deceitful
Familiar, free
Fictitious, counterfeit, false
Fi'gurative, spoken by figure
Formidable, dreadful
Fortúitous, accidental
Fundame'ntal, principal
Ge'nerative, fruitful
Grani'vorous, feeding on grain
Hábitable, that may be dwelt in
Habitual, customary
Harmonious, agreeable
Heretical, containing heresy
Historical, belonging to history
Hónorary, belonging to honour
Horizontal, level
Ho'spitable, friendly
Hydro'pical, dropsical, watery
Illiberal, sparing, ungenerous
Illiterate, unlearned
Illustrious, noble, renowned

I'mitable, to be imitated
Immo'derate, extravagant
Immutable, unchangeable
Impartial, just, equal
Impassable not to be passed
Impatient, nasty
Impenitent, not repenting
Imperial, royal
Imperious, haughty, proud
Impertinent, silly, troublesome
Impetuous, violent
Implacable, not to be appeased
Importunate, troublesome
Impregnable, not to be taken
Improbable, unlikely
Improvident, careless
Inanimate, without life
Incohe'rent, not agreeing
Inco'mpetent, not fit
Incongruous, unfit
Inconsistent, not suiting
Inco'ntinent, unchaste
Incredible, beyond belief
Inculpable, unblameable
Indelible, not to be blotted out
Indepe'ndent, not depending
Indi'fferent, unconcerned
Indurable, that may be endured
Industrious, diligent
Ineffable, unspeakable
Infallible, that connot err
Infectious, apt to infect
Inflexible, not to be bent
Ingenious, sharp, witty
Ingenuous, free, sincere,
Inglorious, dishonourable
Initial, the first of all
Injurious, hurtful
Inoffe'nsive, harmless
Insa'tiate, unsatisfied
Insiduous, treacherous
Intelligent, well informed
Intemperate, immoderate
Intermúral, between two walls
Intráctable, ungovernable
Inviduous, envious
Invincible, not to be overcome
Ironical, sneering
Irresolute, unresolved
Irreverent, unmannerly
Judicious, wise, discreet
Laborious, painful
Lascivious, wanton
Legitimate, lawful, proper
Licentious, rude, disorderly
Litigious, quarrelsome
Loquacious, full of talk
Luxuriant, wanton, abounding
Magnanimous, courageous
Magnificent, stately
Malevolent, full of hatred
Malicious, spiteful
Material, momentous
Mechanical, done by mechanics
Me'ditative, thoughtful
Melancholy, sad, pensive
Mercenary, greedy of gain
Metho'dical, regular, exact
Mi'litary, warlike
Mira'culous, wonderful
Mortiferous, deadly
Munificent, bounteous
Na'vigable, passable for ships
Nece'ssitous, needy
Notorious, publicly known
Numerical, denoting numbers
Obedient, submissive
Obnoxious, offensive
Obsequious, dutiful
Officious, obliging
Omnipotent, all-powerful
Omniprésent, every where present
Omni'scient, all-knowing
O'rdinary, common
Orie'ntal, eastern
Outrágeous, fierce, violent
Pálatable, pleasant to the taste
Paro'chial, of a parish
Particular, proper, peculiar

Parturient, ready to bring forth
Peculiar, particular, singular
Penurious, niggardly, covetous
Péremptory, absolute, positive
Perfi'dious, false, treacherous
Pernicious, hurtful
Perpetual, everlasting
Perspicuous, clear, plain
Political, relating to politics
Posterior, following
Potential, powerful
Prácticable, possible
Precárious, uncertain
Precipitate, violent, hasty
Predominant, ruling over
Pre-existent, being before
Pre'ferable, eligible
Prepárative, tending to prepare
Preposterous, absurd
Prodigious, wonderful
Promiscuous, confused
Prophetical, foretelling events
Propitious, favourable
Provincial, of a province
Prudential, wise
Quadrupedal, four-footed
Quotidian, daily
Rapacious, ravenous
Ra'tional, reasonable
Rebe'llious, disobedient
Reciprocal, mutual
Refractory, unruly, headstrong
Regenerate, born again
Remarkable, worthy of note
Re'putable, of good repute
Respo'nsible, able, answerable
Restorative, able to recruit
Re'vocable, that may be repealed
Rheto'rical, eloquent
Sacraméntal, relating to a sacrament
Sati'rical, sharp, severe
Schismatical, separated, divided
Se'asonable, done in season
Sedentary, sitting
Sedi'tious, factious
Sententious, short, energetic
Se'parable, that may be separated
Septe'nnial, of seven years
Sexennial, of six years
Siderial, starry
Significant, clear, expressive
So'ciable, friendly
Solitary, lonesome
Soli'citous, full of care
Sophistical, captious, deceitful
Spi'ritual, divine
Sponta'neous, free, voluntary
Subordinate, inferior
Subservient, serving under
Substantial, solid, wealthy
Superior, uppermost, chief
Susceptible, capable of impression
Suspicious, distrustful
Symbolical, typical
Sympathe'tic, tender
Tempe'stuous, stormy
Te'mporary, for a time
Tena'cious, holding fast
Terrestrial, earthly
Theatrical, scenical
To'lerable, that may be endured
Tri'butary, subject to
Trie'nnial, of three years
Tumultuous, riotous
Tyrannical, like a tyrant
Unanimous, being of one mind
Unive'rsal, general
Uxo'rious, very fond of a wife
Va'luable, of great price
Variable, changeable
Venerable, worthy of reverence
Verna'cular, natural
Vertiginous, giddy
Vexatious, troublesome
Vindictive, revengeful
Vo'luntary, free, willing
Volúptuous, given to pleasure

Voracious, greedy
Vulnerable, that may be [wounded
Warrantable, justifiable
Well-favoured, beautiful

TABLE IX.

VERBS OF FOUR SYLLABLES, ACCENTED AND EXPLAINED.

Abbréviate, to make short
Abominate, to abhor
Accelerate, to put forward
Administer, to supply, to gov- [ern
Adulterate, to mix
A'lienate, to estrange from
Alléviate, to ease, to assuage
Annihilate, to bring to nothing
Anticipate, to prevent
Appropriate, to claim, to set apart
Assimilate, to counterfeit
Associate, to join with
Calumniate, to slander
Capacitate, to make capable
Capitulate, to come to terms
Chăracterize, to describe
Coágulate, to congeal
Commemorate, to celebrate
Commiserate, to take pity on
Conciliate, to reconcile
Confederate, to join together
Congratulate, to rejoice with
Co-operate, to work together
Corroborate, to strengthen
Debilitate, to weaken
Degenerate, to grow worse
Denominate, to give name to
Denunciate, to threaten publicly
Depopulate, to unpeople
Depreciate, to undervalue
Dilucidate, to make clear
Discontinue, to leave off
Discriminate, to distinguish
Dissatisfy, to displease
Diversify, to make different
Enumerate, to reckon up
Evacuate, to empty
Evaporate, to fly off
Exhilerate, to make cheerful
Extenuate, to mitigate
Illuminate, to enlighten
Inaugurate, to invest, to instal
Incorporate, to mix together
Inebriate, to make drunk
Infatuate, to bewitch
Ingeminate, to double
Ingratiate, to get into favour
Inoculate, to ingraft
Insinuate, to give a hint of
Intoxicate, to make drunk
Invalidate, to make void
Méliorate, to make better
Monópolize, to engross
Necessitate, to compel
Negotiate, to traffic
Obliterate, to blot out
Predestinate, to decree
Premeditate, to contrive
Preponderate, to outweigh
Prevaricate, to quibble
Prognosticate, to foretell
Re-edify, to rebuild
Remunerate, to recompense
Reverberate, to beat back

PART IV.

WRITING PIECES, HYMNS, AND PRAYERS.

ALPHABETICAL COPIES.

A COVETOUS man is never satisfied.
Abundance, like want, ruins many.
By diligence and care, you may learn to write fair.
Be wise and beware, and of blotting take care.
Command you may your mind from play.
Contentment is the best fortune.
Duty, fear, and love, we owe to God above.
Demonstration is the best way of instruction.
Every plant and flower, sets forth god-like power.
Examples oft prevail, when arguments do fail.
Fair words are often followed by foul deeds.
Frugality and industry are the hands of fortune.
Godliness, with contentment, is great gain.
Get what you get honestly, and use it frugally.
He that swims in sin, will sink in sorrow.
He is always poor, who is never contented.
It is good to have a friend, but bad to want one.
It is too late to spare, when all is spent.
Judge not of things by their outward appearance.
Keep at a distance from all bad company.
Knowledge of God is the best kind of knowledge.
Learn to live as you would wish to die.
Learning will stand your friend when riches fail.
Many think not of living till they are near dying.
Many are led by the nose more than by their understanding
Nothing is certain in this uncertain world.
Never study to please others to ruin yourself.
Opportunity lost cannot be recalled.
Omitting to do good, is the committing of evil.
Poverty and shame wait upon the slothful.
Provide against the worst, and hope for the best.
Quiet-minded men have always peace within.
Repentance comes too late when all is spent.
Remember thy Creator in the days of thy youth.
Sin and sorrow are constant companions.
Some go fine and brave, only to play the knave.
Those who do nothing, will soon learn to do ill.
Those ne'er can be wise, who good counsel despise.
Use soft words and strong arguments.
Union and peace make discord cease.

Vice is always attended with sorrow.
Virtue is our guiding star to true reason.
Wanton actions are very unseemly.
We dance well when Fortune plays.
Xenophon counted the wise man happy.
Youth is full of disorder, and age of infirmity.
Your delight and care should be to write fair.
Zeal in a good cause, deserves great applause.
Zeal, when blind, is religious gunpowder.

VERSES ON VARIOUS OCCASIONS.

1. ADVICE.

Learn to contemn all praise betimes,
For flattery is the nurse of crimes:
With early virtue plant thy breast;
The specious arts of vice detest.

2. CUSTOM.

Ill customs, by degrees, to habits rise;
Ill habits soon become exalted vice:
Ill customs gather by unseen degrees,
As brooks make rivers, rivers swell to seas.

3. EDUCATION.

Youth, like soften'd wax, with ease will take
Those images that first impressions make:
If those are fair, their actions will be bright;
If foul, they'll clouded be with shades of night.

4. FRIENDSHIP.

Tell me, ye knowing and discerning few,
Where I may find a friend, both firm and true,
Who dares stand by me when in deep distress,
And then his love and friendship most express.

5. FRUGALITY.

Nor trivial loss nor trivial gain despise;
Mole-hills, if often heap'd, to mountains rise.
Weigh ev'ry small expense, and nothing waste;
Farthings, long sav'd, amount to pounds at last.

6. GAMING.

All cheats at games keep gaping for their prey,
Quarrels create, and mischiefs follow play;
It loses time, disturbs the mind and sense,
While oaths and lies are oft the consequence,
And murder, sometimes, follows loss of pence.

7. HONESTY.

Convince the world that you are just and true,
Be just in all you say, and all you do:
Whatever be your birth, you're sure to be
A man of the first magnitude to me.

8. IDLENESS.

The first physicians by debauch were made;
Excess began, and Sloth sustains the trade.
By work our long-liv'd fathers earn'd their food;
Toil strung their nerves, and purify'd their blood.

9. INDUSTRY.

Flee sloth, the canker of good sense and parts,
Of health, of wealth, of honour, and of arts;
Those that court Fame must not their senses please
Her chariot lags when drawn by Sloth and Ease.

10. LEARNING.

From art and study true content must flow,
For 'tis a god-like attribute to know.
He most improves who studies with delight,
And learns sound morals while he learns to write.

11. PRIDE.

Of all the causes which conspire to blind
Man's erring judgment, and misguide the mind,
What the weak head with strongest bias rules,
Is *pride*, the never-failing vice of fools.

12. RELIGION.

Religion prompts us to a future state,
The last appeal from fortune and from fate;
Where God's all-righteous ways will be declar'd,
The *bad* meet punishment, the *good* reward.

13. SWEARING.

Of all the nauseous complicated crimes,
That both infect and stigmatize the times,
There's none that can with impious oaths compare,
Where vice and folly have an equal share.

14. VIRTUE.

Virtue's the chiefest beauty of the mind,
The noblest ornament of human kind;
Virtue's our safeguard, and our guiding star,
That stirs up reason when our senses err.

SENTENCES IN PROSE.

1. Action keeps both soul and body in health; but idleness corrupts and rusts the mind and the understanding: thus, a man of good natural parts and great abilities, may, by sloth and idleness, become so mean and despicable, as to be an incumbrance to society, and even a burden to himself.

Aurelius often used to say, that he would not part with that little he had learnt for all the gold in the world; and that he had more satisfaction from what he had read and written, than from all the victories he had won, and all the realms he had conquered.

2. Be always cautious of that man's company who has no regard to his own reputation; for it is evident, if he values not his own, he will never mind yours.

Be always ready to communicate any thing to your friend that may improve his mind and his morals. Knowledge, like wealth, is a talent given us of God; and, as we have nothing but what we receive from him, we should imitate his love to us, by being always ready and willing to communicate his gifts to others.

Be very cautious of believing little tales and ill reports of others; and far more cautious of reporting them; lest, upon strict inquiry, they should prove false; and then shame will not only attend thee for thy folly, but thy conscience will accuse thee of an act of injustice.

3. Children, like young twigs, may be bent any way; therefore, all who have the care of them, should instil into their little minds early notions of piety and virtue, as they naturally will grow as they are fashioned.

Compare the miseries on earth with the joys of heaven, and the length of one, with the eternity of the other: then will the journey seem short, and your trouble little.

4. Discretion does not show itself in words only, but in all the circumstances of action: in short, it is the handmaid of Providence, to guide and direct us in all the common concerns of life.

Do as much good as you can to mankind in general, as well to your enemies as to your friends; and what is not in your power, pray God to do for them.

5. Education, grounded on good principles, teaches us not to be overjoyed in prosperity, or too much dejected in adversity. It will not suffer us to be dissolute in our pleasures; and will keep us in our anger from being transported to a fury that is brutal.

Every man is fond of happiness: and yet how few are there

that consider their eternal welfare! this plainly shows how our corrupt nature is at variance with itself.

6. Friendship may very properly be called the child of love and esteem; for it is a strong tie, and an habitual inclination, between two persons, to promote the real good and happiness of each other.

Few take care to live well, but many to live long; though it is in a man's power (in all moral duties) to do the former, but in none to do the latter.

7. Good-nature is beneficence accompanied with good sense: is is the product of right reason, which always gives allowance for the common failings of others, by considering that there is nothing perfect in mankind.

God gives us the greatest encouragement to be good, by promising us more happiness than we can express, or all the world can afford; and he also declares, that if we continue in sin and disobey him, he will punish us for ever and ever. If, then, neither these promises nor threatenings will do, we are unavoidably lost.

8. Humility is the grand virtue that leads to contentment; for it cuts off both the envy and malice of inferiors and equals, and makes us patiently bear the unjust insults of superiors.

He is not likely to pass his life with much ease who gives heed to every thing he hears; therefore, every wise man will take care that such dissonant sounds shall go no further than in at one ear and out at the other.

9. Idleness and sloth, like vultures, eat up our health; for if we look back upon the lives of our forefathers, we shall find that their vigour was owing to their exercise, sprightliness, industry, and activity.

Ingratitude must be a very great sin, as it is quite contrary to the nature of that Divine Being who always delights in mercy, and whose vengeance always follows such as repay evil for good.

10. Knowledge fills the mind with entertaining views, and administers to it a perpetual series of gratifications. It gives ease to solitude, fills a public station with suitable abilities, and, when mixed with complacency, adds lustre to those who are possessed of it.

Keep such company as you may improve, or that may improve you: and if you or your companions cannot make one another better, rather leave than grow worse by them.

11. Lying may be thought convenient and profitable, because not so soon discovered; but pray remember, the evil of it is perpetual: for it brings a person under everlasting jealousy

and suspicion; so that they are not to be believed when they speak the truth, nor trusted when perhaps they mean honestly.

Labour not only to know what you ought, but to practise it; and be always ready to make others better by your good advice; at least be very careful not to make them worse by your bad example.

12. Make the study of the sacred scriptures your daily practice and principal concern; and embrace the doctrines contained in them as the real oracles of God, and the dictates of that spirit which cannot lie.

Moral virtues themselves, without religion, are cold, lifeless, and insipid: and it is very evident, that the latter far surpasses the former; for a man may be moral and not religious, but no man can be truly religious without being moral.

13. Never try to be diverting without being useful; say nothing that may offend a chaste ear, nor suffer a rude jest to intrude upon good manners; for the practice of indecency not only discovers wickedness, but even the very want of common sense.

Never try to make confusion by telling tales, nor be an officious witness between parties; it is time enough when you are asked, and then remember always to speak the real truth; and let not power, or fear, or any thing, bias you to tell a known and wilful lie, to please or prejudice either.

14. Opportunity lost cannot be recalled; therefore it is the highest wisdom in youth to make all the sensible improvements they can in their early days; for a young overgrown dunce seldom makes a figure in any branch of learning in his old days.

15. Pleasure and recreation are really necessary to relax our minds and bodies from too much labour and constant attention; but then they should be such as are innocent as well as diverting.

Pitch upon such a course of life as is excellent and praiseworthy, and custom will soon make it both easy and delightful.

16. Quiet-minded men have always peace within; for though the natural passions of human nature do accompany them, yet they are always calm and easy, because they are ever content with the dispensations of Divine Providence.

Quarrelsome people are always at war; and they are often captious and contentious, even in the most inoffensive company; so that it is a great mark of wisdom (for once) to let them have their own way; but it will still be a greater sign of wisdom, so to mark them as not to be abused a second time.

17. Religion, of itself, never hinders us from any duty; for

it actually makes men in public affairs more serviceable; it makes governors apter to rule with a good conscience; and inferiors, for conscience' sake, more willing to obey.

Riches, state, and supremacy, can procure us only a customary respect, and make us the idols of an unthinking crowd; while knowledge and learning will always recommend us to the love of such as are in a superior class, who always esteem the merit of a man's understanding far more than the bare sound of birth and fortune.

18. Superiority, softened with complacency and good breeding, makes a man equally beloved and admired; but being joined to, and mixed with, a severe and morose temper, it makes a man more to be feared than respected.

Some people are lost for want of good advice; others for want of giving good heed to it; and some there are who take up a resolution beforehand never to mend.

19. The duty of parents, masters, and guardians, is to infuse into the untainted youth early notions of justice and honour; that so the advantages of good parts may not take an evil turn, or be perverted to base and unworthy purposes.

There is no safety or security in wicked company, where the good are often made bad, and the bad always worse; i your business indeed call you into such company, go you must; but take care to get away as soon as you can.

20. Useful attainments, in your early days, will procure you great advantage in maturity, of which reading, writing, and arithmetic are amongst the greatest.

Use the gifts and blessings of Providence with so much prudence and caution, that they may not tempt you to forget yourself, or despise your inferiors; and consider, while you enjoy so much, how little you deserve.

21. Vicious men may divert us, and crafty men betray us, for their own interest; but it is only among sober, wise, and just men that we can find friendship, and a lasting entertainment.

22. We often rise above each other in the esteem of the world, according to the real want or advantage of a liberal education.

We may as well expect that God should make us rich without industry, as make us good without our constant endeavours.

23. Xenophon commended the Persians for the prudent education of their children, because they would not suffer them to effeminate their minds with idle and ridiculous stories· being fully convinced of the danger of adding weight to the bias of corrupt nature.

24. You may as well feed a man without a mouth, as give good advice to one who has no disposition to receive it, and whose bent and inclination is only to wickedness.

MORNING HYMN.

AWAKE, my soul, and with the sun
Thy daily stage of duty run;
Shake off dull sloth, and early rise
To pay thy morning sacrifice.

Redeem thy mispent moments past,
And live this day as if thy last,
Thy talents to improve take care;
For the great day thyself prepare.

Let all thy converse be sincere,
Thy conscience as the noon-day clear;
For God's all-seeing eye surveys
Thy secret thoughts, thy works, and ways.

Wake, and lift up thyself, my heart,
And with the angels bear thy part;
Who all night long unwearied sing
High glory to th' eternal King!

EVENING HYMN.

GLORY to thee, my God, this night,
For all the blessings of the light;
Keep me, O keep me, King of kings,
Beneath thy own almighty wings!

Forgive me, Lord, for thy dear Son,
The ill that I this day have done;
That with the world, myself, and thee,
I, ere I sleep, at peace may be.

Teach me to live, that I may dread
The grave as little as my bed;
Teach me to die, that so I may
Rise glorious at the awful day.

O let my soul on thee repose!
And may sweet sleep mine eye-lids close—
Sleep, that shall me more vigorous make,
To serve my God, when I awake.

FOR CHRISTMAS-DAY.

WHILE shepherds watch'd their flocks by night,
All seated on the ground,
The angel of the Lord came down,
And glory shone around.
"Fear not," said he, (for mighty dread
Had seiz'd their troubled mind),
"Glad tidings of great joy I bring
"To you and all mankind.
"To you, in David's town this day,
"Is born of David's line
"The Saviour, who is Christ the Lord;
"And this shall be the sign:
"The heavenly babe you there shall find,
"To human view display'd,
"All meanly wrapt in swathing bands,
"And in a manger laid."
Thus spake the seraph, and forthwith
Appear'd a shining throng
Of angels, praising God, and thus
Address'd their joyful song:
"All glory be to God on high,
"And to the earth be peace;
"Good-will henceforth from heav'n to men,
"Begin and never cease."

FOR EASTER DAY.

JESUS Christ is risen to day,
Our triumphant holiday;
Who did once upon the cross,
Suffer to redeem our loss..
Hallelujah
Hymns of praise then let us sing
Unto Christ our heavenly King;
Who endur'd the cross and grave,
Sinners to redeem and save.

PRAYERS FOR LITTLE CHILDREN.

MORNING PRAYER.

ALMIGHTY God, the Maker of every thing in heaven and earth; the darkness goes away, and the day-light comes at thy command: thou art good, and thou doest good continually.

I thank thee that thou hast taken such care of me this night, and that I am alive and well this morning. Save me, O God, from evil all this day long, and let me love and serve thee for ever, for the sake of Jesus Christ thy Son. *Amen.*

[At five years old, the Child may be taught to repeat the following:]

Bestow on me every good thing that I have need of for my body and my soul: assist me by thy Holy Spirit to do thy will: make me always afraid to offend thee, and let me live and die in thy favour.

Hear the prayer of a child, O Lord, and pardon all my sins, because thy beloved Son died once on earth for sinful creatures, though he never sinned himself, and now he lives in heaven to pray for them, and save them: let his name be praised for ever and ever. *Amen.*

EVENING PRAYER.

O LORD God, who knowest all things, thou seest me by night as well as by day I pray thee, for Christ's sake, forgive me whatsoever I have done amiss this day, and keep me safe all this night while I am asleep. I desire to lie down under thy care, and to abide for ever under thy blessing, for thou art a God of all power and everlasting mercy. *Amen.*

At five years old, the Child may be taught to repeat the following:

Bless all my friends as well as myself, do good to them at all times and in all places, and help me always to serve them in love. And when I have done thy will here, by thy grace assisting me, and enjoyed thy blessings on earth, then give my soul a place in heaven to dwell with thee there, and with thy Son Jesus Christ: for heaven and earth, and all things in them, are thine for ever and ever. *Amen.*

MORNING PRAYER FOR THE LORD'S DAY.

SUFFER me not, O Lord, to waste this thy day in sin and folly; but let me worship thee with much delight. Teach me to know more of thee, and to serve thee better than ever I have done before, that I may be fitter to dwell in Heaven where thy worship and service are everlasting. *Amen.*

EVENING PRAYER FOR THE LORD'S DAY

O MOST gracious God, let me never forget the many good things that I have heard this day: but let them abide in my heart, so as to amend my life, that I may be able to give a good account of them to Jesus Christ our Lord and Saviour, when he comes to judge the world at the last day. *Amen.*

PRAYER ON ENTERING CHURCH.

ASSIST us, O Lord, in these our prayers and supplications; and grant that those things which we ask faithfully, we may obtain effectually, through Jesus Christ our Lord. *Amen.*

WHEN THE SERVICE IS ENDED.

THANKS be to thy holy name, most gracious God, for this opportunity of attending thy public service; and grant, O Lord, that neither our inattention or want of devotion, may render our imperfect petitions unacceptable in thy sight, through Jesus Christ our Lord. *Amen.*

GRACE BEFORE MEAT.

I ENTREAT Thee, O Lord, that the good things which I eat and drink, may keep me alive, and make me able to do Thee some service, for the sake of Jesus Christ thy Son and our Saviour. *Amen.*

GRACE AFTER MEAT.

I THANK Thee, O Heavenly Father, for my daily food, and for every blessing thou bestowest on me: accept my thanksgiving or Christ's sake. *Amen.*

THE SEVEN STAGES OF LIFE.

FIRST STAGE. *Eccles.* ch. xi. v. 10.—Miserable man, in whom, as soon as the image of God appears in the act of his reason, the devil and his own wicked nature blot it in the corruption of his will; for no sooner are we come to our speech, and begin to have a little sense and discretion in discerning things, but we are kept under the fear of the rod and correction

SECOND STAGE. *Eccles.* ix. 9.—We are now apt to think ourselves much happier in this stage than the last, because at fifteen or sixteen years, youth think they are capable of taking the reins in their own hands, and guiding themselves. But know, O youth, thou art in a most piteous situation, and the most dangerous stage of life: thou art now entering into the affairs of the world, which will entrap thee in a cloud of miseries; and thou hast not discretion enough of thyself to avoid many of them.

THIRD STAGE. *Job*, v. 7.—We are apt, in manhood, to think ourselves completely happy, because we are now our own masters, and are not under that immediate command, as before. But, alas! what now are we much better in? The world still allures us with pleasures, the devil tempts us to sin, and we are now far from being quiet and easy.

Fourth Stage. *Prov.* iii. 13.—This stage of life is also attended with perpetual troubles; and there is no real happiness here: for, look backward, and thou art presented with the wickedness of thy youth, the folly of thy childhood, and the waste of time in thy infancy.

Fifth Stage. *Eccles.* vii. 8.—Now the folly of our youth, and the abuse of our time press hard upon us; and happy is he who can now look back upon the pleasure of a well-spent life; for the house now becomes full of cares, the field full of evil, the country full of rudeness and melancholy, and the city full of fashion. Wealth we see envied, poverty contemned, vice is advanced, simplicity derided, and religion ridiculed.

Sixth and Seventh Stages. *Ps.* xc. 10, 12.—Gray hairs are worthy of honour when the behaviour suits; but it is shocking to see an old man take pleasure in sin, and repeat his former follies with delight, while he carries on his head the infallible tokens of his approaching mortality; for when he comes to those years that his eyes grow dim, ears deaf, visage pale, hands shaking, knees trembling, and feet faltering, then it is evident the dissolution of his mortal tabernacle is near at hand.

THE UNIVERSAL PRAYER.

Father of all! in every age,
In every clime ador'd
By saint, by savage, and by sage,
Jehovah, Jove, or Lord!
Thou great First Cause, least under-
Who all my sense confin'd [stood
To know but this that thou art good
And that myself am blind;
Yet gave me in this dark estate,
To see the good from ill:
And binding nature fast in fate,
Left free the human will.
What conscience dictates to be done
Or warns me not to do, [shun,
This teach me more than hell to
That more than heaven pursue.
What blessings thy free bounty gives
Let me not cast away;
For God is paid when man receives:
To enjoy is to obey.
Yet not to earth's contracted span
Thy goodness let me bound,
Or think thee Lord alone of man,
When thousand worlds are round.
Let not this weak unknowing hand
Presume thy bolts to throw,
And deal damnation round the land
On each I judge thy foe.
If I am right, thy grace impart
Still in the right, to stay:
If I am wrong, O teach my heart
To find the better way.
Save me alike from foolish pride,
Or impious discontent,
At aught thy wisdom has denied,
Or aught thy goodness lent.
Teach me to feel another's woe,
To hide the fault I see;
That mercy I to others show,
That mercy show to me.
Mean tho' I am, not wholly so,
Since quicken'd by thy breath:
O lead me wheresoe'er I go,
Through this day's life or death.
This day be bread and peace my lot;
All else beneath the sun,
Thou know'st if best bestow'd or not
And let thy will be done.
To Thee, whose temple is all space,
Whose altar, earth, sea, skies!
One chorus let all beings raise,
All nature's incense rise!

KINGS AND QUEENS SINCE THE CONQUEST.

Kings and Queens.	*Born.* A. D.	*Began their Reign.*	*Reigned.* Y.	M.	D.	*Age.*
William the Conqueror	1027	1066, Oct. 14	20	10	26	60
William Rufus	1057	1087, Sept. 9	12	10	24	43
Henry I.	1058	1100, Aug. 2	35	4	0	77
Stephen	1105	1135, Dec. 1	18	10	2	49

THE LINE OF PLANTAGENET, OR ANJOU.

Henry II.............	1134	1154, Oct. 25	34	8	12	55
Richard I.	1156	1189, July 6	9	9	0	43
John	1166	1199, April 6	17	6	13	50
Henry III.	1207	1216, Oct. 19	56	0	28	65
Edward I.............	1239	1272, Nov. 16	34	7	21	67
Edward II.	1284	1307, July 7	19	6	13	43
Edward III...........	1312	1327, Jan. 13	50	4	27	65
Richard II.	1366	1377, June 21	22	3	8	33

THE LINE OF LANCASTER.

Henry IV.............	1367	1399, Sept. 29	13	5	22	46
Henry V.	1389	1413, Mar. 20	9	5	11	33
Henry VI.	1421	1422, Aug. 31	38	6	4	49

THE LINE OF YORK

Edward IV.	1442	1461, Mar. 4	22	1	5	41
Edward V.	1471	1483, April 9	0	2	15	12
Richard III.	1443	1483, June 22	2	2	0	42

THE FAMILIES UNITED.

Henry VII.	1457	1485, Aug. 22	23	8	0	52
Henry VIII.	1492	1509, April 22	37	9	6	55
Edward VI.	1537	1547, Jan. 28	6	5	9	16
Mary I.	1516	1553, July 6	5	4	11	42
Elizabeth	1533	1558, Nov. 17	44	4	7	69

THE UNION OF THE TWO KINGDOMS.

James I.	1566	1603, Mar. 24	22	0	3	59
Charles I.	1600	1625, Mar. 27	23	10	3	48
Charles II.	1630	1649, Jan. 30	36	0	7	55
James II.	1633	1685, Feb. 6	4	0	7	67
Mary II.	1662	1689, Feb. 13	5	10	15	32
William III..........	1650	1689, Feb. 13	13	0	22	52
Anne	1665	1702, Mar. 8	12	4	24	49
George I.	1660	1714, Aug. 1	12	10	10	67
George II.	1683	1727, June 11	33	4	3	77
George III.	1738	1760, Oct. 25	59	3	4	81
George IV.	1762	1820, Jan. 29	10	4	25	67
William IV.	1765	1830, June 26				

THE CHURCH CATECHISM

Question. What is your name?

Answer. N. or M.

Q. Who gave you this name?

A. My godfathers and my godmothers in my baptism; wherein I was made a member of Christ, the child of God, and an inheritor of the kingdom of heaven.

Q. What did your godfathers and godmothers then for you?

A. They did promise and vow three things in my name. First, that I should renounce the devil and all his works, the pomps and vanities of this wicked world, and all the sinful lusts of the flesh. Secondly, that I should believe all the articles of the Christian faith. And, thirdly, that I should keep God's holy will and commandments, and walk in the same all the days of my life.

Q. Dost thou not think that thou art bound to believe and to do as they have promised for thee?

A. Yes, verily; and by God's help, so I will. And I heartily thank our heavenly Father, that he hath called me to this state of salvation, through Jesus Christ our Saviour. And I pray unto God to give me his grace, that I may continue in the same unto my life's end.

Catechist. Rehearse the articles of thy belief.

A. I believe in God the Father Almighty, maker of heaven and earth. And in Jesus Christ, his only Son our Lord, who was conceived by the Holy Ghost, born of the Virgin Mary, suffered under Pontius Pilate, was crucified, dead and buried. He descended into hell; the third day he rose again from the dead: He ascended into heaven, and sitteth on the right-hand of God the Father Almighty; from thence he shall come to judge the quick and the dead.

I believe in the Holy Ghost, the holy catholic church, the communion of saints, the forgiveness of sins, the resurrection of the body, and the life everlasting. Amen.

Q. What dost thou chiefly learn in these articles of thy belief?

A. First, I learn to believe in God the Father, who hath made me and all the world.

Secondly, in God the Son, who hath redeemed me and all mankind.

Thirdly, in God the Holy Ghost, who sanctifieth me and all the elect people of God.

Catechist. You said that your godfathers and godmothers did promise for you, that you should keep God's commandments. Tell me how many there be.

A. Ten.

Q. Which be they?

A. The same which God spake in the twentieth chapter of Exodus; saying, I am the Lord thy God, who brought thee out of the land of Egypt, and out of the house of bondage.

I. Thou shalt have no other gods but me.

II. Thou shalt not make to thyself any graven image, nor the likeness of any thing that is in heaven above or in the earth beneath, or in the water under the earth. Thou shalt not bow down to them, nor worship them: for I the Lord thy God am a jealous God, and visit the sins of the fathers upon the children, unto the third and fourth generation of them that hate me; and show mercy unto thousands in them that love me and keep my commandments.

III. Thou shalt not take the name of the Lord thy God in vain, for the Lord will not hold him guiltless that taketh his name in vain.

IV. Remember that thou keep holy the Sabbath-day. Six days shalt thou labour, and do all that thou hast to do; but the seventh day is the sabbath of the Lord thy God. In it thou shalt do no manner of work; thou, and thy son, and thy daughter, thy man-servant, and thy maid-servant, thy cattle, and the stranger that is within thy gates. For in six days the Lord made heaven and earth, the sea, and all that in them is; and rested the seventh day: wherefore the Lord blessed the seventh day, and hallowed it.

V. Honour thy father and thy mother, that thy days may be long in the land which the Lord thy God giveth thee.

VI. Thou shalt do no murder.

VII. Thou shalt not commit adultery.

VIII. Thou shalt not steal.

IX. Thou shalt not bear false witness against thy neighbour.

X. Thou shalt not covet thy neighbour's house, thou shalt not covet thy neighbour's wife, nor his servant, nor his maid, nor his ox, nor his ass, nor any thing that is his.

Q. *What dost thou chiefly learn by these commandments?*

A. I learn two things; my duty towards God, and my duty towards my neighbour.

Q. *What is thy duty towards God?*

A. My duty towards God is to believe in him; to fear him; and to love him, with all my heart, with all my mind, with all my soul, and with all my strength: to worship him, to give him thanks, to put my whole trust in him, to call upon him, to honour his holy name, and his word, and to serve him truly all the days of my life.

Q. *What is thy duty towards thy neighbour?*

A. My duty towards my neighbour, is to love him as myself, and to do to all men, as I would they should do unto me; to love, honour, and succour my father and mother; to honour and obey the queen, and all that are put in authority under her; to submit myself to all my governors, teachers, spiritual pastors, and masters; to order myself lowly and reverently to all my betters; to hurt nobody by word or deed; to be true and just in all my dealings; to bear no malice nor hatred in my heart; to keep my hands from picking and stealing, and my tongue from evil-speaking, lying, and slandering; to keep my body in temperance, soberness, and chastity; not to covet or desire other men's goods; but to learn and labour truly to get mine own living, and to do my duty in that state of life, unto which it shall please God to call me.

Catechist. My good child, know this, that thou art not able to do these things of thyself, nor to walk in the commandments of God and to serve him, without his special grace, which thou must learn at all times to call for by diligent prayer. Let me hear, therefore, if thou canst say the Lord's prayer.

A. Our Father which art in heaven, hallowed be thy name; thy kingdom come; thy will be done on earth, as it is in heaven. Give us this day our daily bread; and forgive us our trespasses, as we forgive them that trespass against us. And lead us not into temptation, but deliver us from evil. Amen.

Q. What desirest thou of God in this prayer?

A. I desire my Lord God, our heavenly Father, who is the giver of all goodness, to send his grace unto me and to all people; that we may worship him, serve him, and obey him, as we ought to do. And I pray unto God, that he will send us all things that be needful, both for our souls and bodies; and that he will be merciful unto us, and forgive us our sins; and that it will please him to save and defend us in all dangers, ghostly and bodily; and that he will keep us from all sin and wickedness, and from our ghostly enemy, and from everlasting death. And this I trust he will do of his mercy and goodness, through our Lord Jesus Christ; and therefore I say Amen, so be it.

Q. How many sacraments hath Christ ordained in his church?

A. Two only, as generally necessary to salvation; that is to say, baptism, and the supper of the Lord.

Q. What meanest thou by this word sacrament?

A. I mean an outward and visible sign of an inward and spiritual grace, given unto us, ordained by Christ himself, as a means whereby we receive the same, and a pledge to assure us thereof.

Q. How many parts are there in a sacrament?

A. Two; the outward visible sign, and the inward spiritual grace.

Q. What is the outward visible sign, or form in baptism?

A. Water, wherein the person is baptised in the name of the Father, and of the Son, and of the Holy Ghost.

Q. What is the inward and spiritual grace?

A. A death unto sin, and a new birth unto righteousness; for, being by nature born in sin, and the children of wrath, we are hereby made the children of grace.

Q. What is required of persons to be baptised?

A. Repentance, whereby they forsake sin; and faith, whereby they steadfastly believe the promises of God made to them in that sacrament.

Q. Why then are infants baptised, when by reason of their tender age they cannot perform them?

A. Because they promise them both by their sureties; which promise, when they come to age, themselves are bound to perform.

Q. Why was the sacrament of the Lord's supper ordained?

A. For the continual remembrance of the sacrifice of the death of Christ, and of the benefits which we receive thereby.

Q. What is the outward part, or sign, of the Lord's supper?

A. Bread and wine which the Lord hath commanded to be received.

Q. What is the inward part, or thing signified?

A. The body and blood of Christ, which are verily and indeed taken and received by the faithful in the Lord's supper.

Q. What are the benefits whereof we are partakers thereby?

A. The strengthening and refreshing of our souls by the body and blood of Christ, as our bodies are by the bread and wine.

Q. What is required of them who come to the Lord's Supper?

A. To examine themselves, whether they repent them truly of their former sins: steadfastly purposing to lead a new life; have a lively faith in God's mercy through Christ, with a thankful remembrance of his death, and be in charity with all men.

POSTSCRIPT.

As there are many people who cannot read old English print, it may be of service to insert the alphabets and give a single lesson, by which any person may soon learn to read it well.

A B C D E F G H I J K L M N O
P Q R S T U V W X Y Z.
a b c d e f g h i j k l m n o p q r s
t u v w x y z.

If you desire to be really happy, learn first of all to be acquainted with yourself; for if you are unacquainted with your own corrupt nature, it is not likely you should be able to comprehend things far above it. Look then into the glass of your own imperfections, and the true sight and sense of them will certainly lead you to real happiness.

Learn then in your youth to contemn the flatteries of all seeming prosperity, and be so inwardly prepared with a serenity of mind, as not only cheerfully to meet with, but even to overcome the fears of all adversity.

CONCLUSION.

TO THE READER.

Should you learn any thing by what is penn'd
Tho' e'er so little, I have gain'd my end;
And should you know already what is writ,
Pray be not over fond of cens'ring it:
But fairly join the critic and the friend,
Small faults excuse, and what you can, commend;
"For be an author e'er so wise and wary,
"He may in some particulars miscarry."

Advice to Young Persons intended for Trade.

BY DR. BENJAMIN FRANKLIN.

Remember that time is money.—He that can earn ten shillings a day at his labour, and goes abroad or sits idle one half of the day, though he spends but sixpence during his diversion or idleness, ought not to reckon *that* the only expense: he has really spent, or rather thrown away, five shillings besides.

Remember that credit is money.—If a man lets his money lie in my hands after it is due, because he has a good opinion of my credit, he gives me the interest, or so much as I can make of the money during that time. This amounts to a considerable sum where a man has large credit, and makes good use of it.

Remember that money is of a prolific or multiplying nature.—Money can produce money, and its offspring car produce more, and so on. Five shillings turned is six; turned again is seven and three-pence: and so on, till it becomes a hundred pounds. The more there is of it, the more it produces every turning, so that the profits rise quicker and quicker. He that throws away a crown, destroys all that it might have produced, even scores of pounds.

Remember that six pounds a year is but a groat a-day.—For this little sum (which may be daily wasted, either in time or expense, unperceived) a man of credit may, on his own security, have the constant possession and use of a hundred and twenty pounds. So much in stock, briskly turned by an industrious man, produces great advantage.

Remember this saying, "The good paymaster is lord of another man's purse."—He that is known to pay punctually and exactly to the time he promises, may, at any time, and on any occasion, raise all the money his friends can spare. This is sometimes of great use. Next to industry and frugality, nothing contributes more to the raising of a man in the world, than punctuality and justice in all his dealings; therefore never keep borrowed money an hour beyond the time promised, lest a disappointment shut up your friend's purse for ever.

The most trifling actions that affect a man's credit are to be regarded.—The sound of the hammer at five in the morning, or nine at night, heard by a creditor, makes him easy six months longer; but if he sees you at a billiard-table, or hears your voice at a tavern, when you should be at work, he sends for his money the next day, and demands it before it is convenient for you to pay him.

Beware of thinking all your own that you possess, and of living accordingly.—This is a mistake that many people who have credit fall into To prevent this, keep an exact account, for some time, both of your expenses and income. If you take the pains at first to enumerate particulars, it will have this good effect: you will discover how wonderfully small trifling expenses mount up to large sums; and will discern what might have been, and may for the future be saved, without occasioning any great inconvenience.

In short, the way to wealth, if you desire it, is as plain as the way to market. It depends chiefly on two things, *industry* and *frugality*; that is, waste neither *time* nor *money*, but make the best use of both.

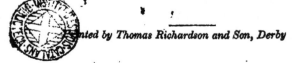

Printed by Thomas Richardson and Son, Derby

Lightning Source UK Ltd.
Milton Keynes UK
UKHW020628230621
386017UK00005B/199